The Little Book of Consciousness:

Holonomic Brain Theory
and
The Implicate Order

Shelli Renée Joye

B.S. Electrical Engineering
M.A. Indian Philosophy
Ph.D. Consciousness Studies

The Viola Institute Inc.
Viola, California

Dedicated to David Bohm and Karl Pribram,
and to all my teachers and mentors, including
John Lilly, Haridas Chaudhuri,
Brian Swimme, Allan Combs, Dean Radin,
Allan Watts, Bede Griffiths,
and to my loving family,
Alyssa, Jason, and Teresa Joye,
and especially to Susanne Rohner
whose careful reviews refined the images and text.

Published in the United States of America
by The Viola Institute Inc.
35366 Wild Turkey Lane
Shingletown, California, USA
www.violainstitute.com

Printed in the United States of America
First Edition

**The Little Book of Consciousness:
Holonomic Brain Theory and
The Implicate Order**.

ISBN-13: 978-0-9988785-4-6 (Pbk)
ISBN-10: 0-9988785-4-5

Cover image by Shelli Renée Joye:
Traditional *Sri Yantra* in egg tempra on wood with gold leaf.

Consciousness is the background, or simply the ground, of all experience. Whatever experience you have, whether it is a high mystical rapture, an abysmal depression, an explosive sexual ecstasy, the sight of a bright twinkling star in a dark night sky, the sound of thunder, the taste of honey, or the scent of sandalwood, it all unfolds in an already dimensionless field of perfect emptiness that is the open shining ground that lurks behind and permeates all of experience. It is consciousness.

Allan Combs, 2009
Consciousness Explained Better

Remember, thought is conditioned reflex at a very high subtle level. It just goes by itself, but it has in it the thought that thought is being produced by a center, which it calls "Me." And all the feelings, which should belong to that center, are thrown onto Consciousness as if from "Me."

David Bohm, 1990
Wholeness and the Implicate Order

CONTENTS

By the same author:

Tuning the Mind - Geometries of Consciousness:
Holonomic Brain Theory and the Implicate Order

"Shelli Joye's integrative masterpiece, *Tuning the Mind*, reads like insane science fiction—quantum black holes, a universal center that's everywhere and nowhere, the dark energy holoflux, and of course, the mysterious Teilhardian isospheres. But the strange thing is, it's not insane, nor is it fiction. It's a novel and refreshing scientific take on the role of consciousness in the physical world. Well worth the read."

——**DEAN RADIN, Ph.D.**,

Chief Scientist, Institute of Noetic Sciences (IONS), and author of
Supernormal: Science, Yoga, and the
Evidence for Extraordinary Psychic Abilities

Introduction

The material offered in this book is an illustrated integration of slides and commentary developed originally in a series of presentations, based upon my doctoral research, published in my dissertation, and subsequently refined over the past two years at the following conferences:

Society for Consciousness Studies Conference,
May 2015, San Francisco, California

Foundations of Mind Conference,
May 2016, Berkeley, California

Science & Nonduality Conference,
August 2016, Titignano Castle, Italy

Science & Nonduality Conference,
October 2016, San Jose, California

Foundations of Mind Conference,
January 2017, San Francisco, California

Science & Nonduality Conference,
August 2017, Titignano Castle, Italy

The approach taken is trans-disciplinary, one that considers and relates established concepts not only from the extensive neurophysiological research findings of Karl Pribram and the ontological understanding of quantum physics developed by David Bohm, but also from readings in philosophy, religion, mysticism, and direct perceptual, introspective, cognitive experience.

We find now, in the early 21st century, that excessive focus and specialization has resulted in a human approach to knowledge that has become increasingly fragmented.

The archetypal pattern of the Tower of Babel comes to mind, with each domain of knowledge speaking its own topical dialect, so replete with jargon and acronyms that the possibilities for cross-discipline dialog have been inhibited and impaired. According to the systems thinker, Edgar Morin, the problem seems to be both fragmentation and lack of integration:

> An influx of knowledge at the end of the 20th century sheds new light on the situation of human beings in the universe. Parallel progress in cosmology, earth sciences, ecology, biology and prehistory in the 1960s and 1970s have modified our ideas about the universe, the earth, life and humanity itself. But these contributions remain disjointed. That which is human is cut up into pieces of a puzzle that cannot form an image. . . The new knowledge, for lack of being connected, is neither assimilated nor integrated. There is progress in knowledge of the parts and paradoxical ignorance of the whole.[1]

The integral approach presented in this book assumes that valid data may be found beyond the traditional methodologies which compartmentalize knowledge. The integral method applied here considers information as valid from multiple and often disparate domains, always with the goal of detecting correlations among them, resonances which might offer new perspectives to clarify our understanding and point to alternate avenues for future research. In order to facilitate the assimilation of the wide range of ideas introduced, the material is presented in a series of 95 slides, one per page, with minimal textual annotation.

---

[1] Morin, *Seven Complex Lessons in Education for the Future*, 21.

In this series of slides we will show that the theories of Bohm and Pribram offer material with which to perceive a wide range of interconnections between neurophysiological research, sub-quantum physics, consciousness, and fundamental maps of the universe. Bohm and Pribram became colleagues, working together from within their different specialties, and together a new picture of consciousness in the universe began to emerge. Their holoflux theory is quite unique yet provides a clear map for those interested in consciousness research, either in the laboratory or through direct experiential exploration using techniques of introspection, prayer, contemplative practices, or entheogenic-fueled psychonautics.

To Bohm, the larger universe, which he referred to as "the Whole," consists of two domains, an unfolding *explicate* order in space-time and a nonlocal (non-temporal, non-spatial) *implicate* order with additional dimensions as predicted by string theory. Bohm concluded that consciousness will eventually be found, not within space-time, but as *primary within the actuality of the implicate order.*

Pribram's forty years of laboratory data supports Bohm's model of the Whole consisting of three hypostases: 1) an *explicate order* (our space-time cosmos), 2) an *implicate order* (at the center of space-time, everywhere, and yet nondual), and 3) a continual *holoflux energy* bridging and communicating with the two orders. The entire Whole, according to Bohm, is continually enfolding and folding between a transcendent implicate order and an immanent explicate order. Pribram's data convinced him that perception and memory follow a holographic Fourier-like transformation process between Bohm's nonlocal implicate order and the brain's explicate, space-time order.

The integrated ideas of Pribram and Bohm present a map and a theory of consciousness that is congruent and coherent with established principles of physics and neurophysiology, while offering a holonomic mind-brain-field hypothesis as a feasible answer to what has been called "the hard problem" of consciousness. This map should be of significant benefit by providing a new understanding of the dynamics experienced in prayer and contemplation, and also act as an aid in navigating the effects of entheogenic psychedelics for those involved in exploring inner space. An Appendix has been included, *The Pribram-Bohm Holoflux Theory*, which discusses, in greater technical detail, the holoflux theory of consciousness.

The Little Book of Consciousness:

A Practical Introduction to Pribram's Holonomic Brain Theory and Bohm's Implicate Order

The material offered in this book was originally developed for a presentation given at the *Science & Nonduality Conference* held at Titignano Castle near Orvieto, Italy in early August 2017.

Here in this book the same 100 visual images and diagrams are used to clarify the approach to a new paradigm for understanding consciousness, the Pribram-Bohm holoflux theory. This new map is fully aligned with the findings of modern physics, mathematical cosmology, and neurophysiology.

Highlighting the essentials of Karl Pribram's *holonomic brain theory* and David Bohm's sub-quantum theory of the *implicate order*, the map of consciousness drawn here may be useful as a guide for contemplative prayer, psychonauts, and entheogenic fueled explorations.

1

Background

- **B.S.E.E.** → Electrical Engineering

- **M.A.** → Philosophy & Religion

- **Ph.D.** → Consciousness Studies

- **Doctoral Dissertation** (2016):
  "The Pribram-Bohm Holoflux Theory of Consciousness:
  An Integral Interpretation of the Theories of Karl Pribram,
  David Bohm, and Pierre Teilhard de Chardin"

  Dissertation Research Committee: Allan Leslie Combs, Ph.D., Chair
  Brian Thomas Swimme, Ph.D.
  Dean I. Radin, Ph.D.

2

But first my background, I have degrees in
Electrical Engineering,
Philosophy & Religion,
and   Consciousness Studies.

All share a common thread
in my early fascination with
science fiction,
consciousness,
and   radio communication.

In short, I was a GEEK !

I learned Morse code and electronics
and had an amateur radio station by age twelve.

With the help of my neighbor, who was a HAM and
who happened to work for the CIA as
an Electrical Communications Engineer,
I built a small working linear ion accelerator

With which i won the Northern Virginia Science Fair
during my senior year in high school, and
which i am sure helped me to be accepted into MIT.

But in college, although i started out in physics and
math, I graduated as an electrical engineer.

However,
the summer before my final year of electrical
engineering
(It happened to be 1967, the "summer of love"),
sometime in July,

I found myself with two friends having taken
a large dose of LSD-25 on a clear star filled night,
on a California beach,
just south of Big Sur.

As I wandered around beneath the stars,
a new and amazing cosmos opened up . . .

I felt I had become one with the Star Maker.

4

RADIANT PLASMA
IN THE BLOODSTREAM

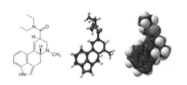

Lysergic Acid
Diethylamide
Efflorescence

My theory is that these amazingly complex
hydrocarbon molecules of lysergic acid
diethylamide, breaking down
in the warmth of a coursing ionic bloodstream,
radiate a unique electromagnetic energy spectrum
which interacts with, resonates with,
and drives the blood's magnetic plasma.

The experience on this California beach,
shortly after my twenty-first birthday,
had suddenly recast my interests from that of
mastering radio communication theory
into a passion for exploring inner space.
My new goal became one of mapping the
relationships between electromagnetic theory,
physics and the experience of consciousness.

5

There are three assertions made in
the Pribram-Bohm holoflux theory of consciousness.

First, consciousness manifests as tunable radiant energy.
Pribram found holonomic information
encoded within electromagnetic flux in the cranium.

Second, that consciousness resonates between two domains,
the space-time *explicate order* and the what the physicist
David Bohm called the *implicate order*, a spaceless, timeless
nondual dimension.

Third, that the source of consciousness
peers out into space and time
from within the implicate order
at sub-quantum dimensions from the CENTER, everywhere,
at the very bottom of space.

6

Bohm's Fascination with Plasma

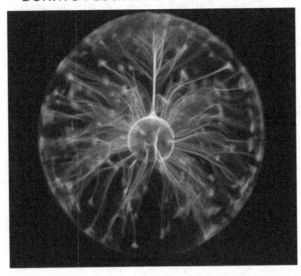

David Bohm, who pioneered the sub-quantum
dimensions of the Implicate Order,
was fascinated with Plasma,
one of the four fundamental states of matter.

His dissertation at UC Berkeley presented an entirely
new mathematical model of plasma.

Plasma Expanding from Supernova

Plasma constitutes over 99% of the matter of the universe, and is the primary constituent of cosmological structures, such as stars and gas clouds.

And for the next 40 years he worked tirelessly, trying to elicit an ontological understanding of the plasma state, And what it might mean for physics, cosmology, and human consciousness.

8

Plasma Emanating from Black Hole'

Bohm's Biographer, David Peat, tells us,

"As Bohm studied the plasmas
he became struck by their extraordinary nature."

Intergalactic Plasma Clouds

At every scale, both microscopic and inter-galactic,
these plasma entities began to take on,
for him,
the qualities of **living beings**

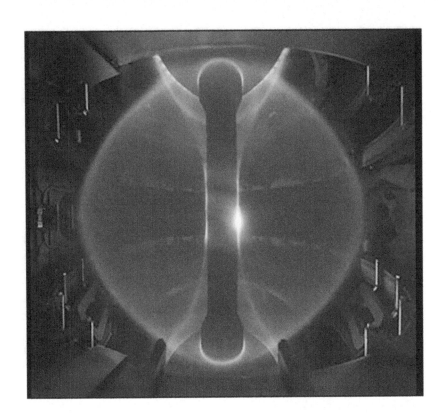

When Bohm introduced an **electrical probe**
into the plasma,
a charged sheath
quickly formed around the intruder,
as if the plasma were protecting itself."

To Oppenheimer's surprise, Bohm put forth
an entirely new theory of the plasma state,
supported with a mathematical model.

Bohm's discovery
was immediately put to use by Oppenheimer
to separate U^{235} from U^{238},
a critical step
in the effort toward building a thermonuclear bomb.

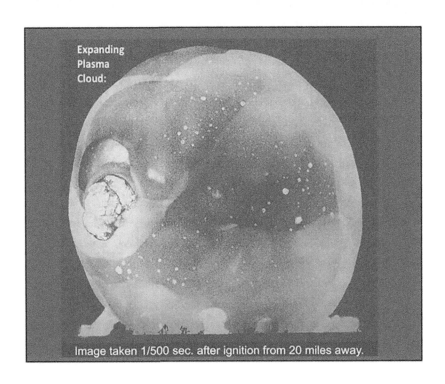

Expanding
Plasma
Cloud:

Image taken 1/500 sec. after ignition from 20 miles away.

At that point Bohm's dissertation was classified **TOP SECRET**
and it was only with considerable effort
that Oppenheimer was able to persuade the University
to grant Bohm a doctorate,
without publishing his dissertation.

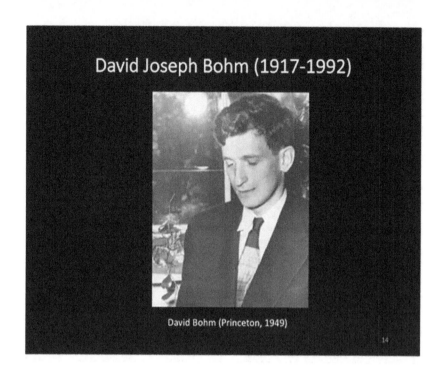

David Joseph Bohm (1917-1992)

David Bohm (Princeton, 1949)

Here we see the young physics professor,
David Bohm,
at Princeton in 1949,
a neighbor and friend of Albert Einstein.

14

At the time Bohm was writing a 600 page textbook,
which he called simply
Quantum Theory,
And which was subsequently published
and widely used in university physics departments.

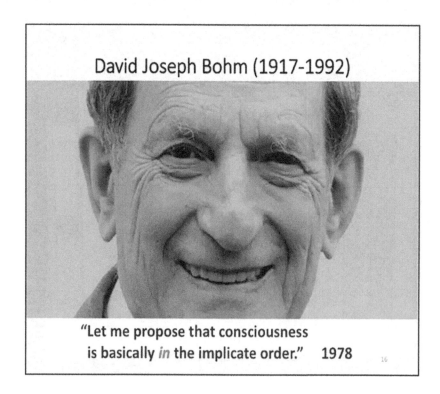

David Joseph Bohm (1917-1992)

"Let me propose that consciousness
is basically *in* the implicate order."   1978

Thirty years later, now Chair of Theoretical Physics
at the University of London,
and after 20 years of metaphysical dialog with
J. Krishnamurti,
Bohm writes:

**"Let me propose
that consciousness is basically in the implicate order."**

So what does Bohm **mean** by the implicate order?

16

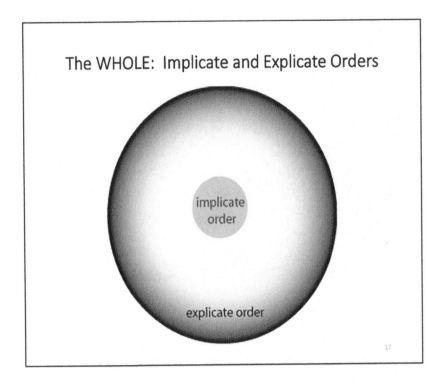

The WHOLE: Implicate and Explicate Orders

implicate order

explicate order

17

Through his mathematical model of plasma,
Bohm had begun to realize
that the Whole of reality
must consist of **two distinct regions**,
an **EXPLICATE ORDER**, which we know as space and time,
and a NONDUAL **IMPLICATE ORDER** which is
beyond space-time.

I'll discuss this in detail.
but first I want to introduce Bohm's colleague in
the development of
the holoflux theory of consciousness.

Karl H. Pribram (1919-2015)

Karl Pribram, 1960

Karl Pribram, 1990

Here we see Karl Pribram, who passed away in 2015 at the age of 95. He was called "The Magellan of the Mind."

Karl, also an emeritus Stanford professor, was the author of well over 700 publications,
and he continued to teach, research, and lecture well into his 90s.

He published his final book, *The Form Within: My Point of View*, in 2013 at the age of 93.

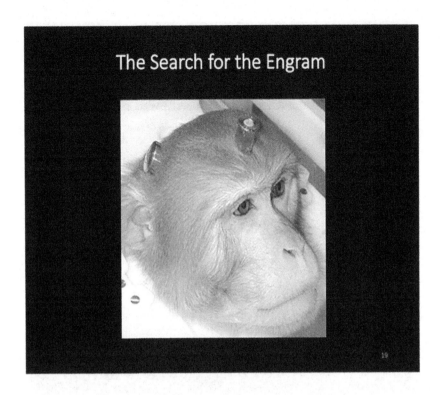

The Search for the Engram

Since the 1940s, Karl had been carrying out experiments in search of the mysterious *engram*, the location of memory storage within the brain.

But he and his colleagues were unable to discover any such specific location.

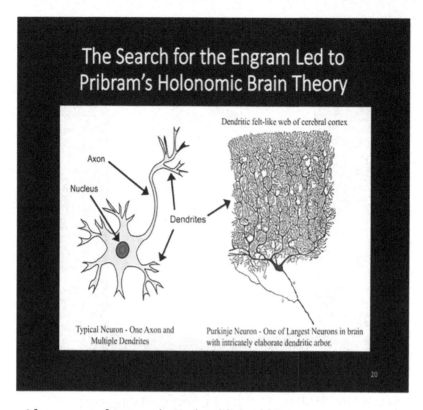

The Search for the Engram Led to Pribram's Holonomic Brain Theory

Dendritic felt-like web of cerebral cortex

Axon

Nucleus

Dendrites

Typical Neuron - One Axon and
Multiple Dendrites

Purkinje Neuron - One of Largest Neurons in brain
with intricately elaborate dendritic arbor.

20

After years of research, Karl published his
HOLONOMIC BRAIN THEORY.

In a long series of experiments, he discovered
three-dimensional electric fields
within the space of the dendritic webs of the cerebral
cortex,
depicted to the right in the figure.

Karl's extensive lab data suggested evidence of holographic
field transformations as the fundamental mechanism in
perception
and provided proof that memories are not stored locally.

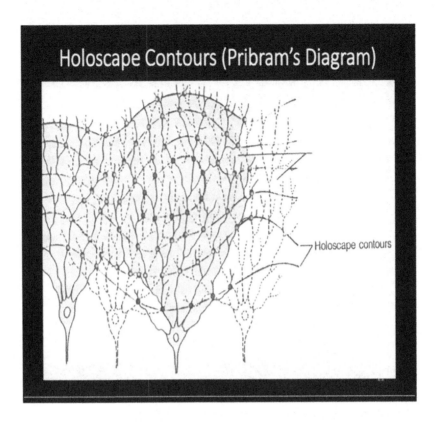

Holoscape contours

In his experiments mapping the effect of visual images from the eye

Pribram discovered that when *values of identical voltage in the brain* are connected, unusual contour maps become apparent.

While not visually congruent with the images being viewed, these patterns are similar in appearance to typical holographic patterns.

He called these patterns, **holoscape contours**.

21

Dynamic Holonomic Brain Patterns

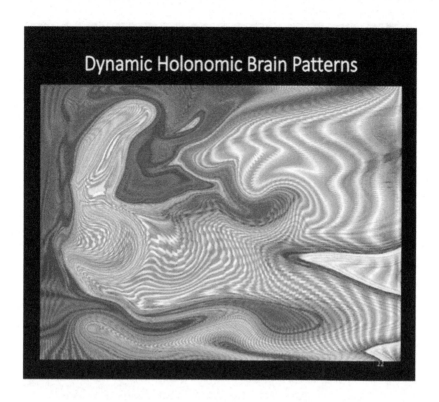

In 1964 Pribram read a paper on holograms,
and immediately noticed
how holographic patterns were similar to
those appearing in the holoscape contours that he had
discovered in the brain.

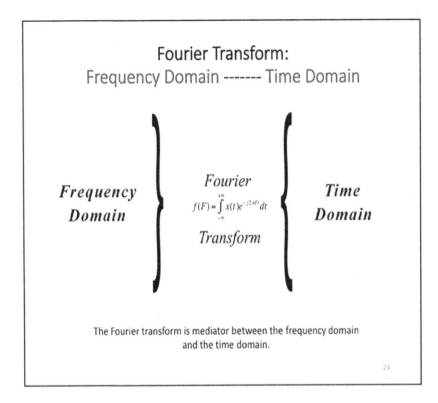

The Fourier transform is mediator between the frequency domain and the time domain.

In the same paper Pribram learned
that the mathematics of the Fourier transform
describe **a natural process** in which there is
A TRANSFORMATION between **TWO dimensions** or **domains**,
the **frequency domain** and **the time domain.**

He began to suspect that brain processing and memory storage might involve
a **non-temporal, non-spatial frequency domain.**

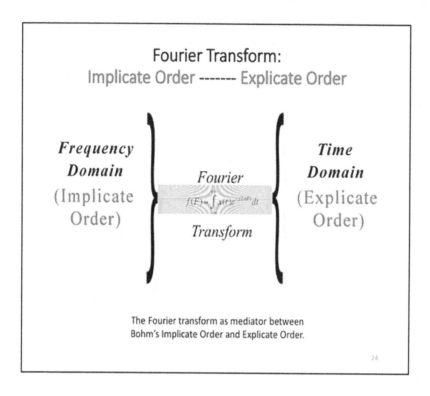

Fourier Transform:
Implicate Order ------- Explicate Order

The Fourier transform as mediator between
Bohm's Implicate Order and Explicate Order.

This became **central** to Karl's holonomic brain theory,

A theory which eventually grew to
include David Bohm's concept of
the Implicate Order
as a **possible** factor in **memory** storage and **perception**.

David Bohm and Karl Pribram

Saral Bohm, David Bohm, Karl Pribram
(Prague, June 1992)

This picture of David Bohm, his wife Saral, and Karl Pribram dining out in Prague, was taken by Karl's wife, Katherine Neville, shortly before Bohm's death in 1992.

Pribram and Bohm,
the quantum physicist and the brain scientist,
had become close friends
over two decades of technical discussion.

---

*Katherine Neville is an internationally acclaimed science fiction writer, who kindly allowed me to use the photograph in my dissertation.

Pribram and Bohm were **both** fascinated by the phenomenon of consciousness.

While Pribram's research revealed a new understanding of the mechanisms of **memory, sight, and hearing in terms of holograms,**

Bohm's work supported Pribram's discoveries by identifying the broad outlines of a **geometry of consciousness** mapping the universe as a **Whole**, including both space-time as well as the **nondual implicate order** frequency domain supported by a new mathematical theory.

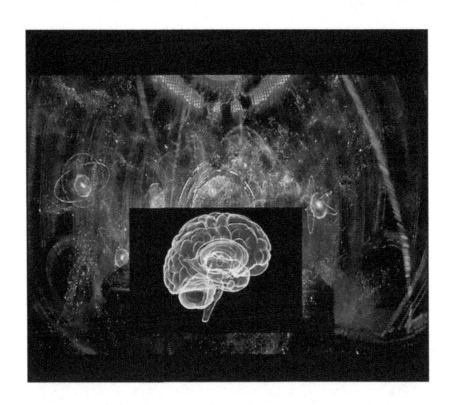

Bohm and Pribram held a common vision of the **hologram** as **key** to understanding consciousness and the brain.

In fact,
David Bohm once said that if our eyes had no lenses, the entire universe would appear as a hologram.

Together they pioneered a theory that is **quite unconventional**, certainly outside of mainstream thought in physics and neurophysiology, and yet their **holoflux theory** is **coherent** and **applicable**
for mapping consciousness and the cosmos.

At the heart of this theory are three cosmological constants,
the **Speed of Light**,
the **Planck Length,** and
the **Planck Time Constant.**

Planck Constants and Speed of Light

Constants	Values
Speed of Light	2.99792×10^8 meters/sec
Planck Length	1.616199×10^{-35} meter
Planck Time	5.39106×10^{-44} seconds

29

The Speed of Light was first measured in 1676 by the Danish astronomer, Olaus Roemer, by observing eclipses of the moons of Jupiter. In 1862 Leon Foucault, using mirrors, measured the speed of light accurately to within 1% of the currently accepted constant.

The other two constants in the chart were discovered by **the father of quantum mechanics, Max Planck,** and first published in his famous paper in 1900 **which began quantum theory**.

Planck used the **speed of light** and the **gravitational constant, to calculate these values.**

The PLANCK LENGTH IS KEY TO HOLOFLUX THEORY.

To better understand
the **Planck length**,
And of the **implicate order itself**
a thought experiment is useful here.

Please focus your attention upon the small sphere
at the center of this diagram,
and assume that it has even smaller dimensions within,
that it has an "inside."

Now lets begin **moving inward, jumping by leaps of 10,**
geometrically, toward the center.

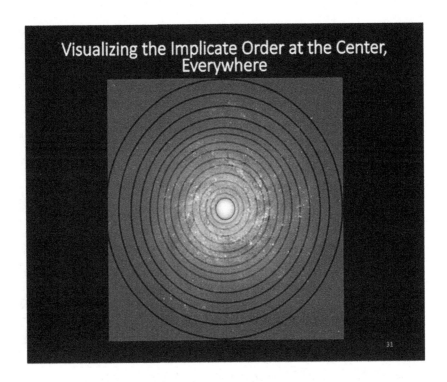

Imagine that as we jump toward the center
we are also **shrinking in scale** by a factor of 10.

With every jump, we are
SHRINKING LIKE ALICE IN WONDERLAND

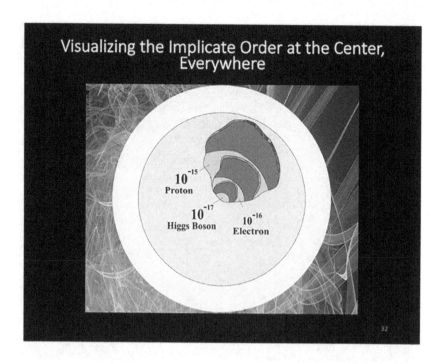

AT JUMP 15 WE find ourselves at 10^{-15} meters, the diameter of a proton.

ONE MORE JUMP INWARD TAKES US TO 10^{-16} meters, the size of an **electron**.

The next jump takes us to 10^{-17} meters, the size of the **Higgs Boson**.

We are now as **deep**
as current measurements can go,
at the limit of the **Large Hadron Collider.**

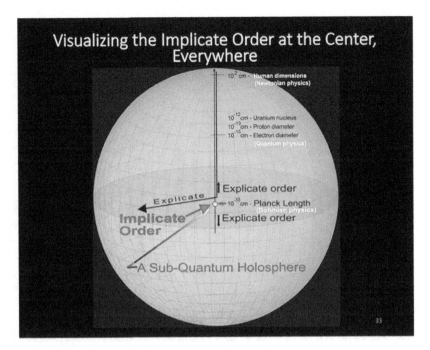

But let us continue shrinking **inwards**,
shrinking ever downwards, toward the center of space,
Moving towards the bottom of the **EXPLICATE ORDER,**
Where space ends.

We find ourselves standing on the surface of a **SUB-
QUANTUM HOLOSPHERE,**
Many billions of times smaller than an electron.

According to physics and the speed of light constant, we can
shrink no further.

This is the end of the line.

We have reached the bottom limit of cosmic reality,
or have we?

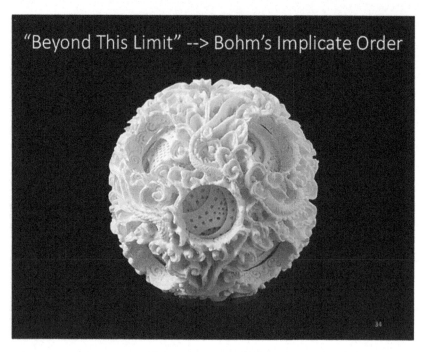

"Beyond This Limit" --> Bohm's Implicate Order

Bohm doesn't think so, and neither do I, and

I quote from
Wholeness and the Implicate Order:

"To suppose that there is nothing **beyond** this limit at all would indeed be quite arbitrary.

Rather, it is very probable that **beyond it** lies a further domain,
or set of domains,
the nature of which
we have as yet little or no idea."

A Holoplenum of Holospheres

A Planck Holosphere

The Holoplenum

Bohm, going even further, tells us that here,
at the bottom of space,
Reality constitutes an actual **plenum***.

BOHM STATES . . .

---

* *"Plenum" – A space that is completely filled.*

"What we perceive through the senses
as empty space is actually the plenum,
which is the ground for the existence
of everything, including ourselves.
The things that appear to our senses
are derivative forms and their true meaning
can be seen only when we consider the plenum,
in which they are generated and sustained,
and into which they must ultimately vanish."
David Bohm

"What we perceive through the senses
as empty space is actually the plenum,
which is the ground for the existence of
everything, including ourselves. The
things that appear to our senses are
derivative forms and their true meaning
can be seen only when we consider the
plenum, in which they are generated
and sustained, and into which they must
ultimately vanish."

Luminiferous (Light-Bearing) Aether Theory
Proposed by Albert Michelson and Edward Morley in 1887

Michelson-Morley

This is **strikingly** reminiscent of the previously discredited *aether* concept,
a core belief of 19th century physics.

A Holoplenum of Holospheres ?

Recalling that Bohm's theory posits consciousness as flux resonance between two domains,
the explicate order and **implicate order**,
the question now arises,

"What is the **relationship** between
the *energy of consciousness* within the **implicate order** and the *energy of consciousness* within the **explicate order?**

What is the **mechanism** of information interchange between the two?

For an answer we turn to the following diagram. . .

38

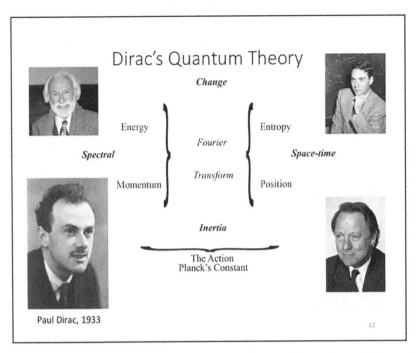

Dirac's Quantum Theory

Change

Energy

Entropy

Fourier

Spectral

Space-time

Transform

Momentum

Position

Inertia

The Action
Planck's Constant

Paul Dirac, 1933

This diagram, appearing in several of Pribram's published works, indicates **the basic relationships** underlying quantum theory.

Pribram obtained this diagram during a presentation given by the head of the Berkeley physics department, **Geoffrey Chew** (upper right).

who told Pribram that he had been given it by another Berkeley physicist, **Henry Stapp** (lower right).

Stapp said that the diagram was authored by the Father of Quantum Physics himself! **Paul Dirac** (lower left).

Central to Dirac's diagram is the **Fourier Transform,**

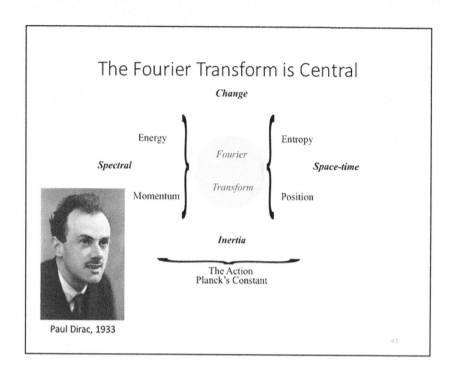

the mathematical bridge between
the **Spectral** and the **Space-Time** domains.

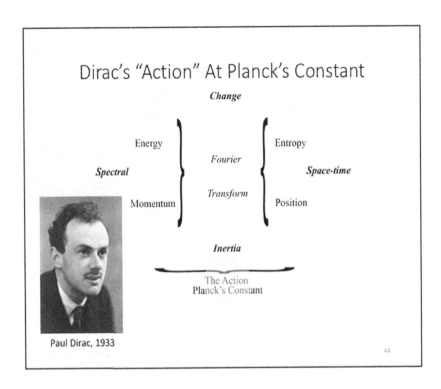

Dirac's "Action" At Planck's Constant

Paul Dirac, 1933

And at the very bottom of the diagram Dirac indicates that it is here,
at the scale of Planck's Constant,
where we find **The Fundamental Action**.

The Fourier Transform

Jean-Baptiste Joseph Fourier

$$f(t) = \int_{-\infty}^{+\infty} X(F)e^{j2\pi F} \qquad\qquad f(F) = \int_{-\infty}^{+\infty} x(t)e^{-j2\pi Ft}dt$$

Fourier integral transform of a continuous frequency function into the time domain.

Fourier integral transform of a continuous time function into the frequency domain (f_d).

A brief review of the Fourier transform is in order.

In 1822, Jean Baptiste Fourier, experimenting with heat flow,
discovered a mathematical transformation
mapping energy in two domains.

The equation on the left transforms information
from the frequency domain
into the time domain.

The equation on the right transforms information
from the time domain
into the frequency domain.

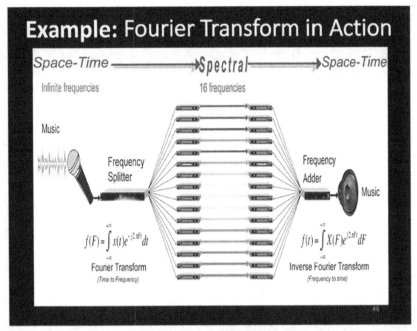

Here we see an engineering application of Fourier Transform processing.

Incoming music is detected by a microphone at the left.

At regular intervals, the acoustic wave
is sliced by a frequency splitter into 16 unique frequencies.

The amplitude of each frequency is recorded and stored.

Thus incoming **Space-Time music** has been converted to **Spectral** data.

The frequency data is then later unpacked, mixed,
and emerges from the speaker at the right, once more in **space-time**.

THE HOLOFLUX HYPOTHESIS posits that *the energy of consciousness* operates in a somewhat similar fashion,
continually transforming between two domains.

43

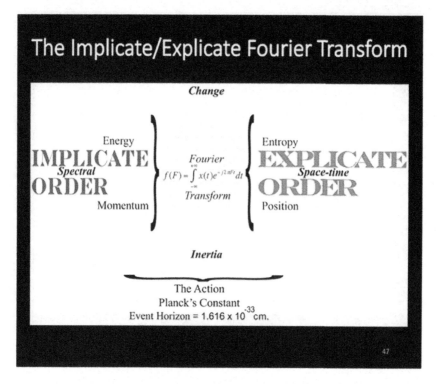

Here we see Bohm's IMPLICATE and EXPLICATE ORDER within the context of Dirac's diagram.

The Implicate Order lies within the SPECTRAL ENERGY REGION.

The Explicate Order lies within Space-Time to the right.

Again, at the **Center** we see the Fourier Transform.

But to fully understand abstract relationships such as these, it is more useful to visualize the relationships geometrically.

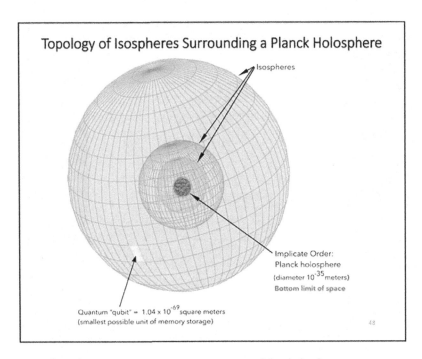

Topology of Isospheres Surrounding a Planck Holosphere

Isospheres

Implicate Order:
Planck holosphere
(diameter 10^{-35} meters)
Bottom limit of space

Quantum "qubit" = 1.04×10^{-69} square meters
(smallest possible unit of memory storage)

In this diagram we see a quantum black hole,
or Planck holosphere,
separating space from an interior Implicate Order.

Surrounding the central Planck holosphere are thin shells
called isospheres, each providing enormous memory
storage capacity.

For simplicity, only three isospheres are shown here,
but in actuality we should consider many,
one for each unique quantum frequency
in the virtually infinite
electromagnetic radiation spectrum.

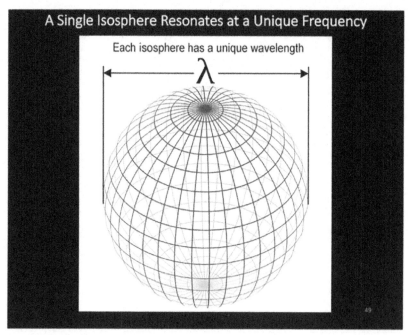

Each isophere has a unique wavelength

λ

From RADIO THEORY, we know that each isosphere must resonate at the unique frequency
constrained by its specific diameter, its **wavelength**.

This unique frequency in the space-time **EXPLICATE ORDER** resonates with
the **IDENTICAL** frequency **within** the **IMPLICATE ORDER.**

This is how CONSCIOUSNESS within the nondual implicate order communicates with electromagnetic energy in our familiar space-time,
THROUGH FREQUENCY RESONANCE via the mathematics of the FOURIER TRANSFORM.

Notice the grid. Each rectangular grid represents ONE bit of information stored on the isosphere. Let me explain.

46

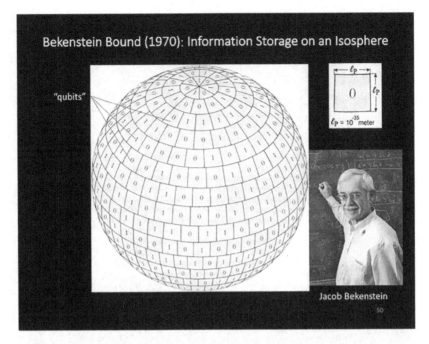

Bekenstein Bound (1970): Information Storage on an Isosphere

"qubits"

$\ell_P = 10^{-35}$ meter

Jacob Bekenstein

As a graduate student under John Archibald Wheeler, who coined the term "black hole,"
Jacob Bekenstein pioneered the mathematics of **black hole thermodynamics.**

Bekenstein defined the **qubit** as the smallest possible storage area
in space, having an area of **one square Planck length.**

The upper limit to the information that can be contained upon the surface of a specific, finite volume of space has come to be known as the
"Bekenstein bound."

And just why is this storage so important?

47

Because, along with
This recent Chinese teleportation experiment,
It implies that the universe may already have
a natural **faster-than-light**
Quantum Communications Network already in place.

In the experiment, photons were beamed
from a station in Tibet
to a Chinese satellite orbiting 300 miles above Earth.

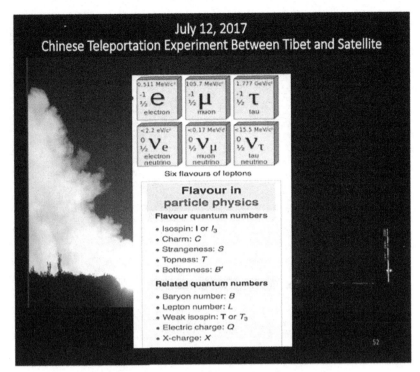

ALL of these quantum particle properties,
including FLAVOUR values of *Charm*, *Strangeness*,
Topness, and *Bottomness*,
were instantaneously transferred from a particle
on the ground
to a particle 300 miles away in orbit around the planet,
faster than the speed-of-light.
IN EFFECT
– supporting the supposition that quantum
TELEPORTATION may indeed by possible through the
nonduality of the quantum black hole plenum below the
Planck length, via Bohm's nontemporal, nonspatial
IMPLICATE ORDER.

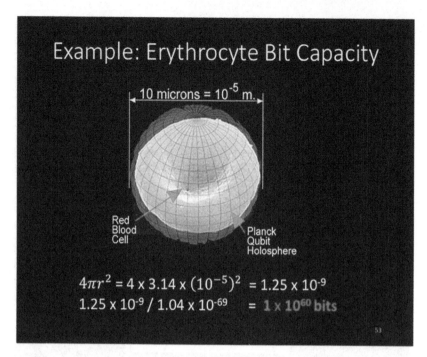

Example: Erythrocyte Bit Capacity

10 microns = 10^{-5} m.

Red
Blood
Cell

Planck
Qubit
Holosphere

$4\pi r^2 = 4 \times 3.14 \times (10^{-5})^2 = 1.25 \times 10^{-9}$

$1.25 \times 10^{-9} / 1.04 \times 10^{-69} = 1 \times 10^{60}$ bits

53

As an example OF HOLONOMIC STORAGE CAPACITY, particularly appealing to those who may consider blood as a possible conveyor of consciousness, let us examine the possible storage capacity of an Erythrocyte, or red blood cell, that mysterious cell
that has **no nucleus and does not reproduce itself,**
is filled with atoms of iron forming a ring, and
yet it is found ubiquitous throughout our body.

If we consider the diameter of a typical erethrocyte, about 10 microns,
the number of bits of information that can be stored on an isosphere bounding such a cell, is 10^{60} bits.

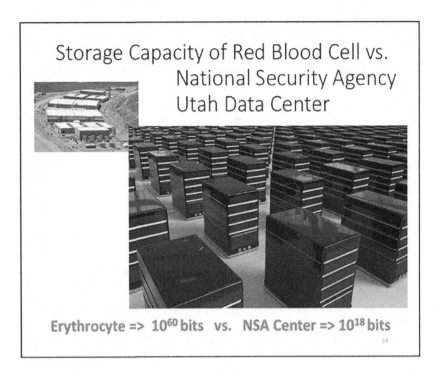

Storage Capacity of Red Blood Cell vs. National Security Agency Utah Data Center

Erythrocyte => 10^{60} bits vs. NSA Center => 10^{18} bits

54

Note that by comparison,
the United States National Security Agency's Utah Data Center has a reported capacity of a mere 10^{18} bits of information.

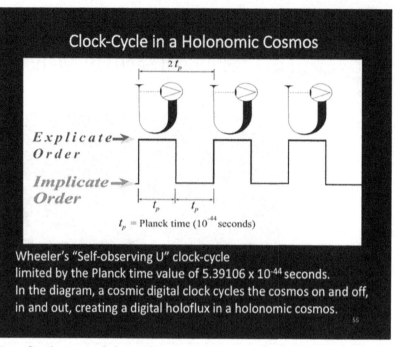

Clock-Cycle in a Holonomic Cosmos

$2 t_p$

Explicate→
Order

Implicate→
Order

t_p t_p

t_p = Planck time (10^{-44} seconds)

Wheeler's "Self-observing U" clock-cycle
limited by the Planck time value of 5.39106 x 10^{-44} seconds.
In the diagram, a cosmic digital clock cycles the cosmos on and off,
in and out, creating a digital holoflux in a holonomic cosmos.

One final piece of the Pribram-Bohm topology concerns the
inclusion of the Planck Time Constant into the equation.
How does the Planck TIME CONSTANT
influence the proposed holoflux process?

Using John Wheeler's famous "Self-Observing U," an image he
often used as short hand to indicate the cosmology of the
universe viewing its own creation,
this slide expresses the fundamental clock-cycle of the cosmos
to be the Planck time of 10^{-44} seconds.

In the diagram, a cosmic digital clock cycles the cosmos
in and out, at a constant rate of the Planck time constant.

This is the digital processing of a holonomic cosmos
at a digital clock rate of
ten to the forty-four pulses per second.

The implications here are enormous!
We can only begin to imagine the cosmos
as we know it
operating at such a clock cycle,

Imagine the entire plenum of galactic matter
collapsing
in and out between the implicate order
and
the explicate order
at a rate of 10^{44} cycles per second.

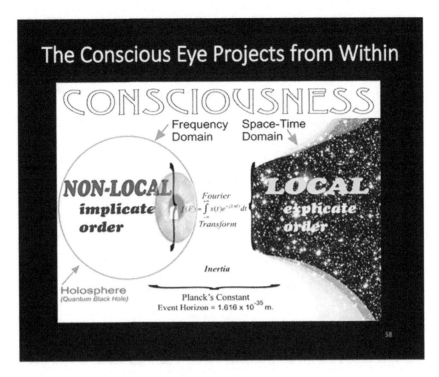

ANOTHER WAY of understanding this theory can be seen here,
AND HAS MAJOR IMPLICATIONS FOR CONSCIOUSNESS,

We have **here** over-laid the image of an **iris**
AT THE SURFACE OF THE
EVENT HORIZON OF AN IMPLICATE ORDER HOLOSPHERE,
TO THE LEFT IN THE DIAGRAM.

WE SEE **consciousness**,
from **within** the nonlocal implicate order
peering **out into** our local space-time **explicate order** of visible stars
and galaxies.

BOHMS SAYS THAT space-time UNFOLDS FROM the IMPLICATE
ORDER, that forms are PROJECTED **out into**
SPACE AND TIME
from **WITHIN** the **IMPLICATE ORDER**.

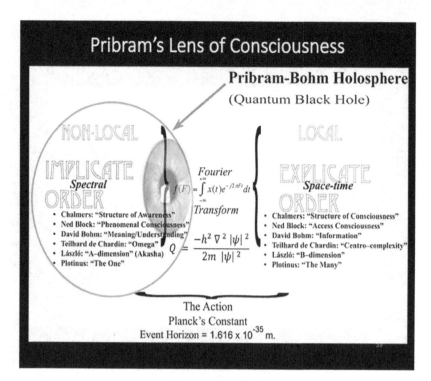

Pribram's Lens of Consciousness

Pribram-Bohm Holosphere
(Quantum Black Hole)

NON-LOCAL

IMPLICATE
Spectral
ORDER

Fourier

$$f(F) = \int_{-\infty}^{+\infty} x(t)e^{-j2\pi Ft}dt$$

Transform

- Chalmers: "Structure of Awareness"
- Ned Block: "Phenomenal Consciousness"
- David Bohm: "Meaning/Understanding"
- Teilhard de Chardin: "Omega"
- László: "A–dimension" (Akasha)
- Plotinus: "The One"

$$Q = \frac{-\hbar^2 \nabla^2 |\psi|^2}{2m |\psi|^2}$$

LOCAL

EXPLICATE
Space-time
ORDER

- Chalmers: "Structure of Consciousness"
- Ned Block: "Access Consciousness"
- David Bohm: "Information"
- Teilhard de Chardin: "Centro–complexity"
- László: "B–dimension"
- Plotinus: "The Many"

The Action
Planck's Constant
Event Horizon = 1.616 x 10^{-35} m.

Bohm's holoflux plasma mathematics
fully supports such a topology.

You can see Bohm's equation for what he called the
QUANTUM POTENTIAL, **Q**, in the center of the diagram,
right below the Fourier Transform and above The Action.

Karl Pribram was in full agreement with Bohm, and
summarizes his own thinking here,
at the age of 94,
and I quote:

"These two domains characterize the input to and output
from a lens
that performs a **Fourier transform.**"

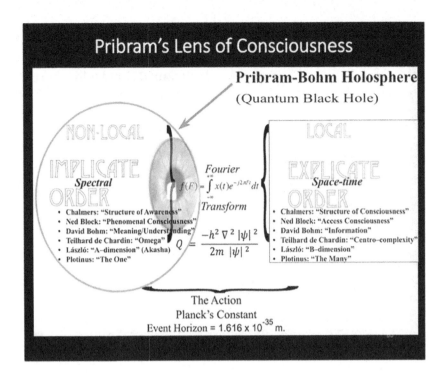

Pribram's Lens of Consciousness

Pribram-Bohm Holosphere
(Quantum Black Hole)

NON-LOCAL

IMPLICATE
Spectral
ORDER

- Chalmers: "Structure of Awareness"
- Ned Block: "Phenomenal Consciousness"
- David Bohm: "Meaning/Understanding"
- Teilhard de Chardin: "Omega"
- László: "A–dimension" (Akasha)
- Plotinus: "The One"

Fourier
$$f(F) = \int_{-\infty}^{+\infty} x(t)e^{-j2\pi Ft}dt$$
Transform

$$Q = \frac{-\hbar^2 \, \nabla^2 \, |\psi|^2}{2m \, |\psi|^2}$$

LOCAL

EXPLICATE
Space-time
ORDER

- Chalmers: "Structure of Consciousness"
- Ned Block: "Access Consciousness"
- David Bohm: "Information"
- Teilhard de Chardin: "Centro–complexity"
- László: "B–dimension"
- Plotinus: "The Many"

The Action
Planck's Constant
Event Horizon = 1.616 x 10^{-35} m.

On one side of the transform lies the space–time order we ordinarily perceive.

Bohm's **Explicate Order**.

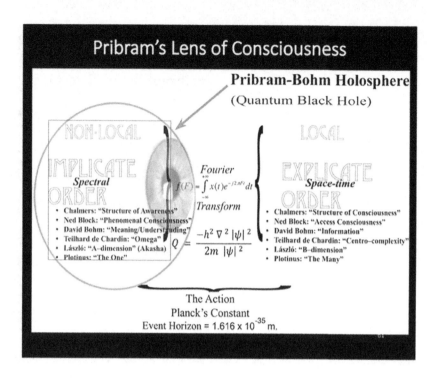

And on the other side lies a distributed enfolded holographic-like order referred to as the frequency or spectral domain," Bohm's **Implicate** .

What might be the implications of the Pribram-Bohm theory, particularly for **consciousness studies, paranormal research, and non-dual experiences**?

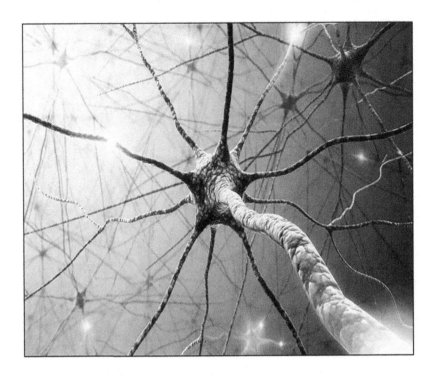

The implications are that consciousness,
the experience itself, is **not** a recent *epiphenomenon*
of some **nerve impulse powered** neuronal process of
the physiological brain.

If we rephrase the famous causality question,
"What came first, the chicken or the egg?" as
"What came first, the brain or consciousness?,"
Pribram and Bohm would answer, "consciousness!"

Panpsychists (many of them scientists) believe that
consciousness predates the brain, that nerve impulse
powered neurons are an *epiphenomenon* of
consciousness, and that *consciousness is everywhere*.

Instead, if we follow the lead of Pribram and Bohm,
consciousness should be regarded as **primary**,
as radiant energy operating lens-like
to focus and tune between the frequency domain and
space-time.

AND WHAT might this imply for a human physiology of
consciousness?

WHERE DO WE LOOK THEN, TO IDENTIFY structures within
the human body
capable of channeling high frequency conscious radiation?

BUT **FIRST** WE NEED TO TAKE A SHORT DIVERSION HERE
INTO THE WORLD
OF RADIO ENGINEERING ANTENNA THEORY.

LET US TAKE A MINUTE

TO REVIEW THE BASIS OF RADIO COMMUNICATION

USING INVISIBLE ELECTROMAGNETIC WAVES.

**THE FUNDAMENTAL LINK INVOLVES
WHAT IS CALLED THE ANTENNA.**

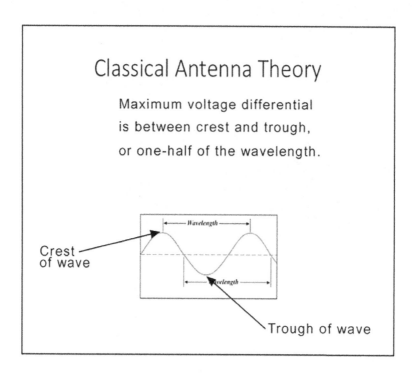

ANTENNA THEORY TELLS US THAT FOR MAXIMUM SENSITIVITY,
BOTH FOR RECEIVING AS WELL AS FOR BROADCASTING,

THE PHYSICAL ANTENNA WAVELENGTH MUST BE **ONE-HALF**
OF THE SIZE OF **THE TARGET FREQUENCY'S WAVELENGTH.**

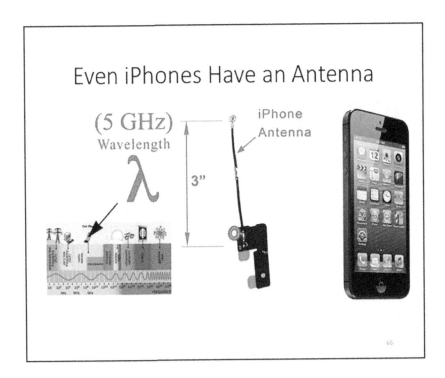

HERE IS AN EXAMPLE

An iPhone signal has a **wavelength**
of approximately 6 inches.

For this reason, the internal antenna of an iPhone
is **one half wavelength, or 3 inches**.

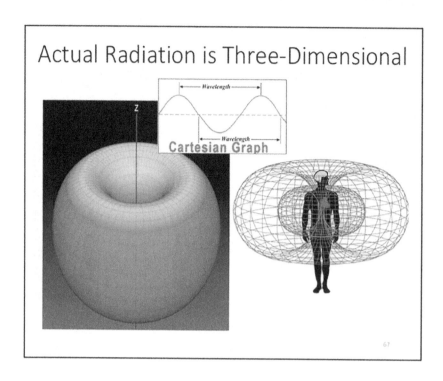

Actual Radiation is Three-Dimensional

Cartesian Graph

BUT THE CARTESIAN LINE **GRAPH OF A SINE WAVE
IS SIMPLISTIC AND MISLEADING.**

ACTUAL RADIATION IS "THREE-DIMENSIONAL,"
AS IT
MOVES OUT FROM THE ANTENNA
OR FROM THE HUMAN HEART
AT THE SPEED OF LIGHT.

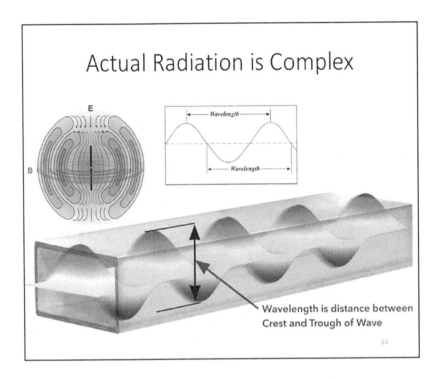

Actual Radiation is Complex

Wavelength is distance between Crest and Trough of Wave

Here are **three different ways** to visualize radiation.

In the upper center we see a typical sine wave drawn in a graph using Cartesian coordinates. Though this is the most common way of depicting a sine wave, found in modern textbooks of mathematics and physics, it is actually quite misleading.

To the left is a more realistic, cross-sectional image of the same sine wave shown in three dimensions. **But along the bottom** we see a view of an electromagnetic sine wave constrained within what is called a **waveguide**.

The diameter of a waveguide acts to guide the wave forward **and** to **protect** it from outside **interference**.

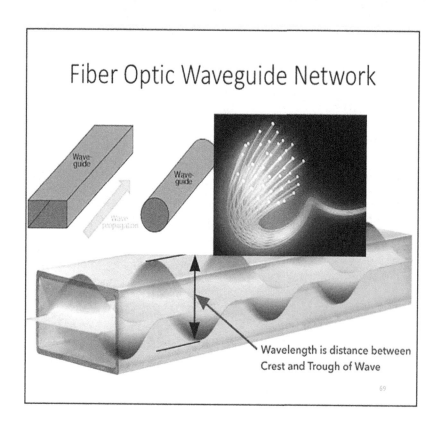

Fiber Optic Waveguide Network

Wave-guide

Wave-guide

Wave propagation

Wavelength is distance between Crest and Trough of Wave

69

THE **INTERNET** IS A NETWORK OF FIBER OPTIC WAVEGUIDES.

THE SUM TOTAL OF INTERNET FIBER OPTIC WAVEGUIDES STRETCHES FOR OVER **550,000** MILES AROUND THE GLOBE.

66

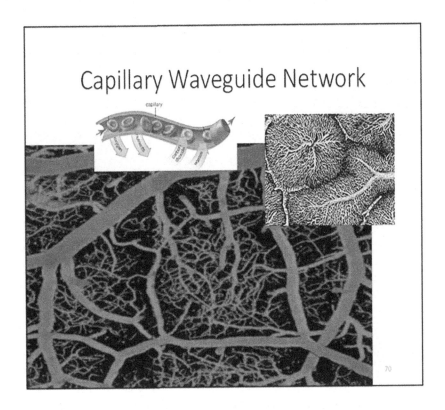

Capillary Waveguide Network

By contrast, the human capillary system
forms a network that
stretching for more than 59,000 miles
throughout the human body (and brain).

It offers a perfect network waveguide
for infrared signals,
and is ideal for 10 microns radiation,
the average diameter of capillaries.

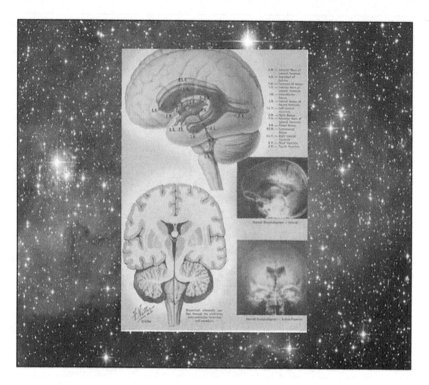

AND this image from a medical textbook
shows the hollow **ventricular cavities**,
filled with clear cerebrospinal fluid.

Medical textbooks say that the only function of these
cavities is to help cushion the brain from trauma impact
due to concussion.

BUT DOES IT SEEM PLAUSIBLE that such beautifully
streamlined shapes, appearing to be
so similar to microwave horn antenna waveguides
should have evolved in the center of the cranium
merely to cushion us from **blows** to the head?

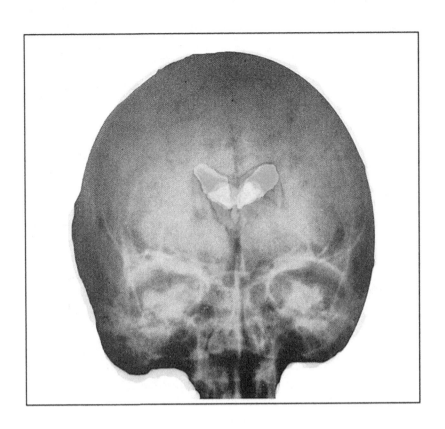

And this x-ray of a human skull
REVEALS THE **WINGED-SHAPE**
OF THE ventricular cavities
AS SEEN FROM THE FOREHEAD.

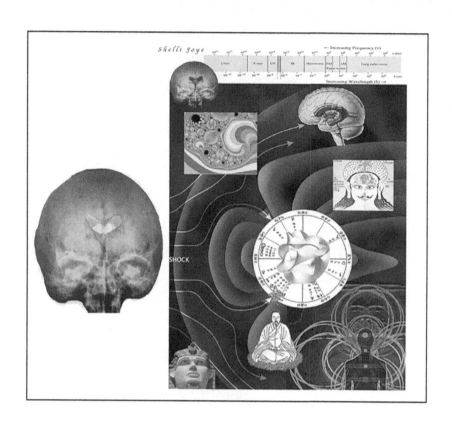

IS IT ONLY A COINCIDENCE
THAT THESE CAVITIES APPEAR
in the **PRECISE** location depicted by
illustrations of **"the third eye,"**
IN EGYPT, CHINA AND INDIA???

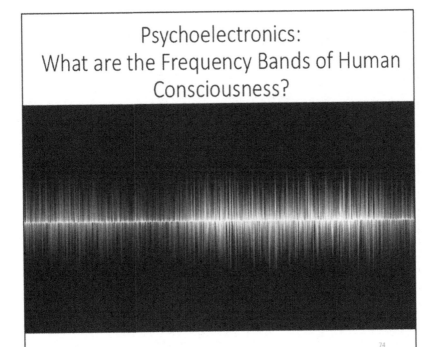

Now if the theory is that thought involves
**tuning the electromagnetic frequencies of the brain
within the human capillary waveguide system,**
the next question must be,
"**Where** might be the various **frequency bands**
to which we might tune our consciousness?"

What are the various ranges and bandwidths of human
consciousness?

This is important both for future research
in the physics of consciousness
as well as for the pioneering efforts of
contemplative exploration by psychonauts.

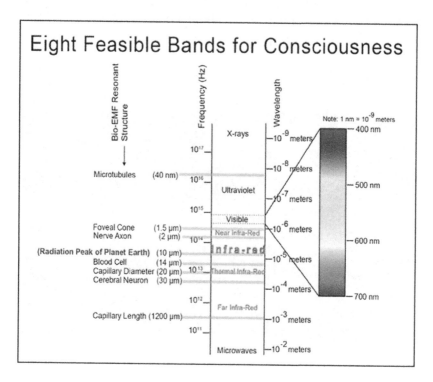

THIS DIAGRAM INDICATES POSSIBLE CHANNELS FOR CONSCIOUSNESS WITHIN THE HUMAN BODY.

Here we compare the size of various structures
To see where electromagnetic wavelengths will
resonate according to antenna theory.

Note that the band of **visible light wavelengths** fall
somewhere in the central range.

At the highest frequencies, we see microtubules providing
waveguides in ultraviolet frequency bands, just slightly
above visible light.

Below the visible light band, we see waveguide possibilities
in blood capillaries channels in the infrared frequency band.

QUANTUM BRAIN DYNAMICS:
The Cortical Field

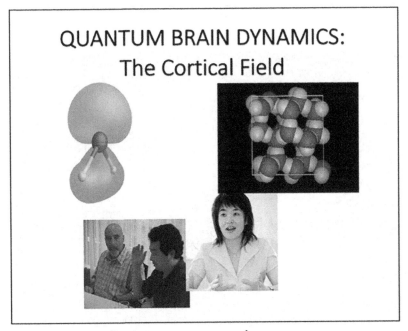

Here we see the Japanese researchers
Mari Jibu, and Kunio Yasue (with Stuart Hameroff).
Jibu and Yasue extended the findings of the physicist
Hiroomi Umezawa to develop
a theory called **Quantum Brain Dynamics** (QBD).

In the 1990s they worked closely with Karl Pribram,
publishing their physiological mathematical theory in an
Appendix to one of Karl's books to provide a sound
mathematical basis for Karl's holonomic brain theory.*

In the upper left is a model of the magnetic field,
generated from **one dipole** of a water molecule.
In the upper left, we see a molecular lattice which
forms a plenum of aligned water molecule dipoles which
offer the basis of what is termed **the cortical field**.

---

* Jibu and Yasue, "A Theory of Nonlocal Cortical Processing in the Brain," in
Pribram's *Brain and Perception: Holonomy and Structure in Figural Processing.*

The Electromagnetic Cortical Field

According to Jibu and Yasue,
the combined electric dipoles
of **all** the water molecules in the
human blood stream
constitute a **single quantum field,**
which resonates within a narrow
band of frequencies in the far infrared.

In this model of consciousness, the human
blood system acts as a **single giant water
molecule resonating as one system of ionic
plasma.**

74

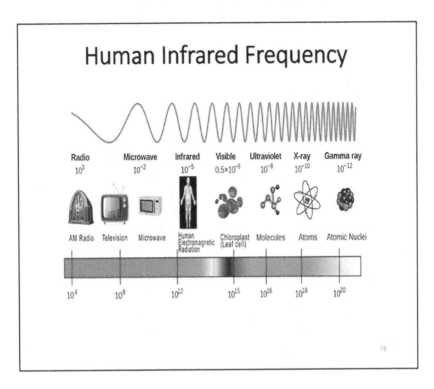

In this figure we can view a small band of the electromagnetic spectrum,
from radio waves at the left to gamma rays on the right.

Note that **as the wavelength become physically smaller**,
(as we see as the axis moving toward the right)
the frequency rate increases.

The physical size of a wavelength is inversely proportional to the frequency.

Higher frequencies, capable of encoding more information, are found at smaller dimensions.

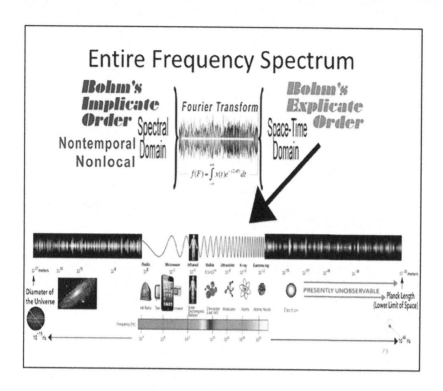

Here we view the same range of frequencies in the explicate order's electromagnetic waves inserted into the center of the **entire FREQUENCY SPECTRUM RANGE OF THE UNIVERSE,** which can be seen here ranging from the diameter of the entire universe at the far left end of the scale (at value of 10^{27} meters),

down to the tiny Planck length limit (10^{-35} meters) located at the right end of the scale.

In terms of frequency, the universe ranges from 10^{-19} Hz to 10^{44} Hz.

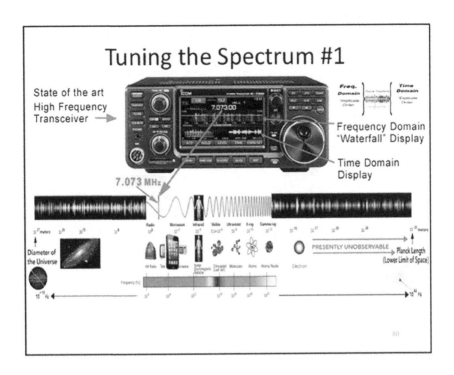

Tuning the Spectrum #1

This is a typical modern communications
radio transceiver, used both
to receive and **to transmit** electromagnetic energy,
but only within a very small range of the vast
electromagnetic spectrum.

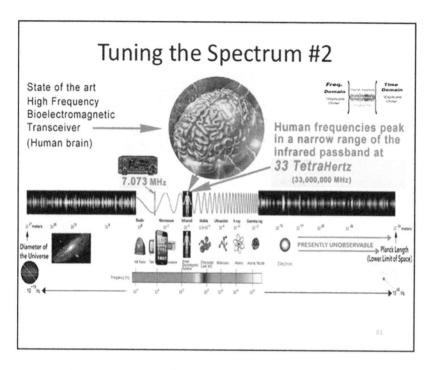

By contrast, Pribram's holonomic brain,
viewed as a transceiver,
may be tuned to the infrared band,
just below the visible light frequencies.

Human infrared peaks at 33 Terahertz,
much higher than radio frequencies.
offering rich computational bandwidth
for thought, sound processing,
and image visualization.

But what **evidence** do we have
that the human brain might operate
in the infrared band region?

78

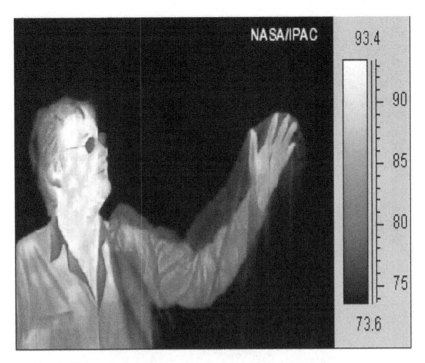

NASA/IPAC 93.4

90

85

80

75

73.6

First of all, humans **glow** with **infrared frequencies.**

This is a photograph of electromagnetic energy radiating from the human body, as seen through "night vision goggles" tuned to the infrared band of electromagnetic radiation.

With an output of 860 watts the human body **glows** with electromagnetic energy. Unfortunately, this phenomenon is commonly dismissed as "heat," even by the scientifically trained, though *heat* is actually only the *human sensory interpretation* of radiant **electromagnetic energy** in the infrared frequency band, high above the radio and microwave frequency bands, having the capacity of handling immeasurably more information than radio waves.

The **scale** on the right **plots temperature** vs **luminosity** according to **Wien's Law.**

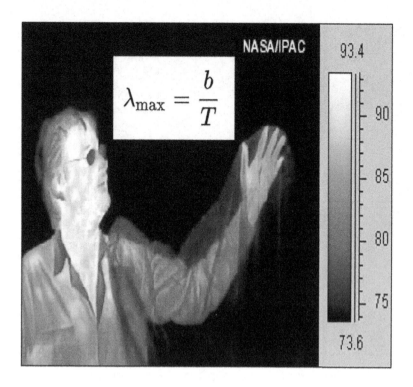

Wien's law is an equation that states that
the MAXIMUM WAVELENGTH
of electromagnetic radiation varies with the inverse of the
temperature. In other words, the higher the temperature,
the smaller the wavelength.

With this equation we can calculate
the **peak wavelength**
radiating at **any given** specific temperature *T.*

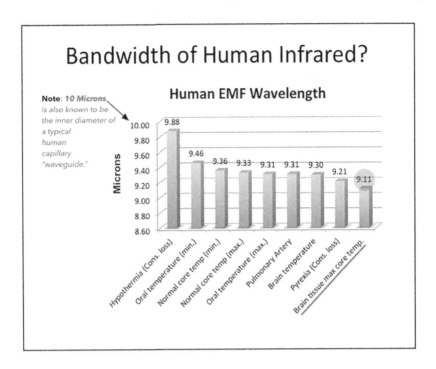

SO WHAT MIGHT BE THE
BANDWIDTH OF HUMAN INFRARED RADIATION?

Applying Wien's Law
at the location of various internal body temperatures,
this chart reveals
the bandwidth of human infrared
to lie close to 10 microns.

In terms of frequency this is
in the 33 Terahertz frequency band, ideal for
high speed information, image, audio, and thought
processing.

Human Electromagnetic Power

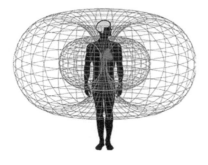

	Output Power
Energy radiated by most powerful radio on the planet	1,500,000 watts
Energy radiated by nuclear reactor (Three Mile Island @ maximum)	873,000 000 watts
Energy radiated by human heartbeats (combined @ 7 billion)	9,100,000,000 watts

In terms of power,
each human heartbeat radiates
a total of **1.3 watts** of infrared electromagnetic energy.

An **iPhone** transmits **1.6 watts** of electromagnetic energy.

And the most powerful radio on the planet broadcasts
a maximum of **1.5 million watts**.

But by contrast,
the combined output of 7 billion human heartbeats is
an astounding
9.1 Gigawatts of electromagnetic infrared power
broadcasting into the noosphere, continuously.

Resonance in the Thermosphere?

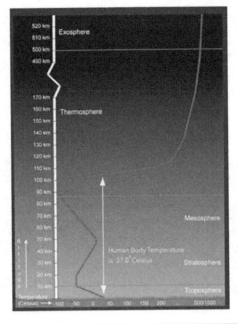

In this graph
we see temperature at various distances from the ground.

Notice how temperature
at first **decreases** as we rise in altitude,

But for reasons not well understood,
the temperature increases sharply above 90 km

At 100 kilometers above sea level the atmospheric
temperature passes through a zone that mirrors
human body temperature at 37 degrees Celsius.

Resonance in the Noosphere?

Could cavity resonance in the thermosphere
be the locus of what Teilhard de Chardin
and Vladimir Vernadsky
termed the **Noosphere***?

---

* In the theory of Vernadsky, the **Noosphere** is the third in a
succession of phases of development of the Earth, after the
Geosphere (inanimate matter) and the Biosphere (biological life). For
Teilhard de Chardin, the Noosphere is the sphere of thought encircling
the earth that has emerged through evolution as a consequence of
this growth in complexity/consciousness.

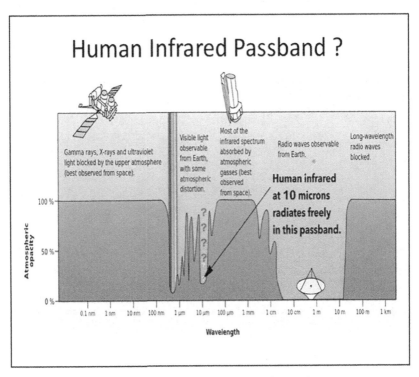

Human Infrared Passband ?

Gamma rays, X-rays and ultraviolet light blocked by the upper atmosphere (best observed from space).

Visible light observable from Earth, with some atmospheric distortion.

Most of the infrared spectrum absorbed by atmospheric gasses (best observed from space).

Radio waves observable from Earth.

Long-wavelength radio waves blocked.

Human infrared at 10 microns radiates freely in this passband.

Atmospheric opacity

100 %

50 %

0 %

0.1 nm   1 nm   10 nm   100 nm   1 μm   10 μm   100 μm   1 mm   1 cm   10 cm   1 m   10 m   100 m   1 km

Wavelength

The atmosphere is opaque and **blocks** radiation at most wavelengths.

However this plot reveals major **passbands** in atmospheric opacity.

As we all can attest, nature has evolved human organs of perception for **the passband** we call **visible light.**

But what about the distinct passband shown here at around 10 micron, the human infrared range?

Human Passband ?

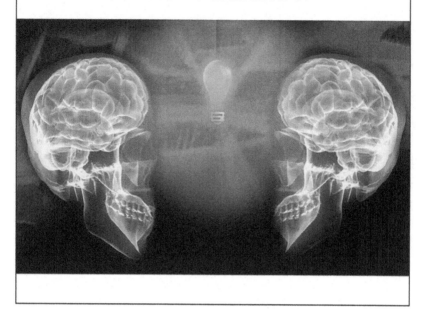

What **organs of perception** might nature have evolved to take advantage of the passband at 10 microns?

Could this be the doorway to regions explored by mystics, yogis, shamans, and saints, and psychonauts throughout recorded history?

Let us take a moment to consider what these ideas imply.

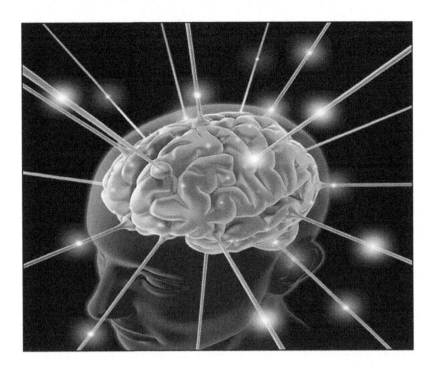

The neocortex is in a way like a personal computer

We can learn
to turn down its activities of verbalization and memory.

We do this in order to allows the deeper consciousness
to become aware of supersensible and normally
inaccessible regions of awareness.

By halting the normal flow of thoughts and memory,
we can suspend our normally active neuronal
biocomputer, putting it into sleep mode.

Only then can we begin to perceive what is beyond
the normal waking boundaries of awareness.

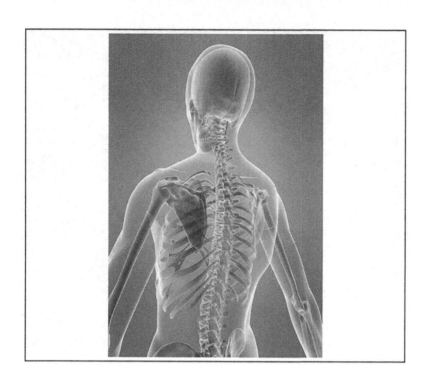

Among those who practice silent contemplation
to explore consciousness, among the
monks, shamans, mystics, and psychonauts,
one widely reported experience is a feeling of
electromagnetic energy that is often
perceived to be rushing upwards,
moving up along the central channel of the spine.

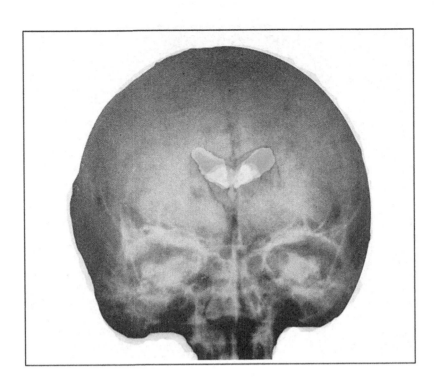

Recalling our x-ray of the ventricular cavities
we see that they are in the **exact** location depicted
by occult illustrations of "the third eye'
experienced by contemplatives,
and called in Sanskrit the
Brahmarandra **or "the cave of Brahma."**

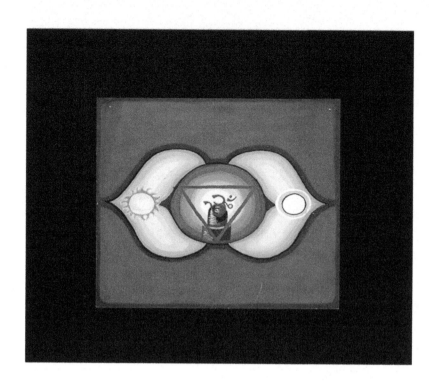

Here we see a
12th century Kashmiri diagram of **the third eye**,
appearing to be the same shape and in the same location as
the **ventricular cavities**
which we saw through the forehead x-ray.

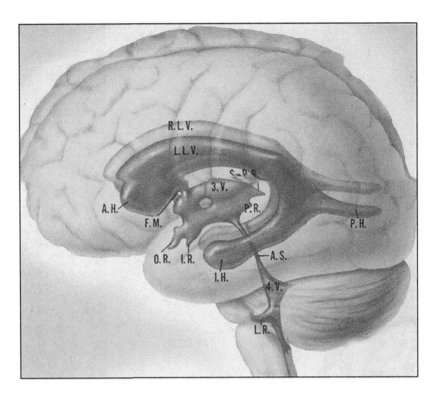

During normal waking activity,
when the cerebral hemispheres are electrically active,
the deeper inner areas are **shielded**
due to
the **Faraday cage effect**.

In a Faraday cage
the moving electrical charges on the outer regions shield
the inner regions.

However when the cortex is silent, such as during sleep,
or during silent contemplation,
the ventricular cavities
are suddenly open to signals coming through
from the outside universe.

Another diagram from Rajasthan showing the third eye chakra at the location of the ventricular cavities.

Also depicted here is the heart chakra.

The heart has been and continues to be
An important center for practicing and developing focus of consciousness.

In fact,
there are **innumerable** locations within the human body that can be developed through contemplative practices such as yoga, Hesychasm, or psychonautic exercises.

This diagram shows many areas within the body
that can be cultivated through
Samyama, according to the instructions found in the classic text on contemplative practices, Patañjali's *Yoga Sutra*.

Patañjali tells us that, after quieting the normal monkey activity of the brain/mind, one should focus upon an internal physiological center such as the heart or the abdomen, or the fontanelle at the top of the head, and by sustaining the concentration for a period of time, new sensations will be evoked and the center will grow in sensitivity, eventually allowing supersensible capabilities (in Sanskrit called *siddhis*) to develop.

This image is taken from an ancient scroll book on Taoist Chinese meditation.

According to the Taoist texts,
when the mind is sufficiently stilled,
the **true self** is seen to rise out of the cranium through the fontanelle and travels up and out to commune with the living cosmos,
perhaps tuning in
to what
Teilhard de Chardin referred to as
"the evolving noosphere."

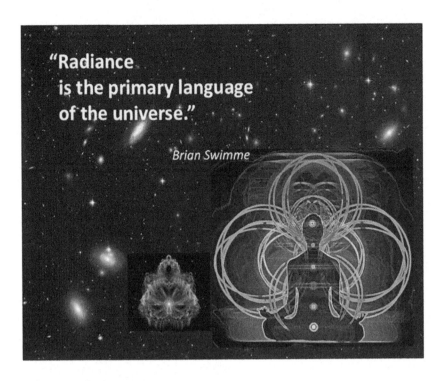

"Radiance
is the primary language
of the universe."

Brian Swimme

In closing, I would like to share
a relevant quote from my mentor
and fellow explorer,
the mathematical cosmologist
Brian Swimme, who has often said

"RADIANCE IS THE PRIMARY LANGUAGE OF THE UNIVERSE"

About the Author

Shelli Renée Joye was born on the island of Trinidad in the British West Indies, and grew up in London and northern Virginia. Accepting a scholarship in Physics from Rice University, she completed a Bachelor of Science in Electrical Engineering. After working with Dr. John Lilly in research involving interspecies communication between dolphins and humans, she began a lifelong exploration of the interface between consciousness, yoga, electromagnetic theory, and mathematics.

She was awarded an M.A. in Asian Philosophy from the California Institute of Asian Studies under the guidance of the founder, Dr. Haridas Chaudhuri, and published a Master's thesis, "The History, Philosophy, and Practice of Tantra in South India." In the early '90s she studied with Fr. Bede Griffiths at Shantivanam in South India.

Dr. Joye completed a Ph.D. program in the Philosophy, Cosmology, and Consciousness program at the California Institute of Integral Studies under the guidance of Drs. Allan Leslie Combs, Brian Swimme, and Dean Radin. She currently lives in a cedar cabin in the Cascade mountains near Lassen forest in northeastern California.

About the Viola Institute

The Viola Institute is a non-profit corporation established to promote consciousness research and to foster an integral, ecumenical, science-based approach to spiritual traditions, contemplative practices, and the numinous arts. To this end, the Institute sponsors art exhibitions and publishes works of nonfiction around the themes of contemplative practice, comparative religion, and consciousness studies. A primary goal of the Viola Institute is to develop two consciousness research and retreat centers, one in northern California near Lassen Volcanic National Park, and the second in a forested rural valley near Assisi, Italy. For more information, or to make a tax deductible contribution contact:

The Viola Institute
35366 Wild Turkey Lane
Viola, CA 96088

Appendix:
The Pribram-Bohm
Holoflux Theory

In the physics of the Pribram-Bohm hypothesis, the larger universe, which Bohm referred to as "the Whole," consists of two domains, an implicate order and an explicate order (*Wholeness and the Implicate Order*, 1980). Pribram's explicate order is congruent with what is referred to in physics as space-time, sensed by human beings through the qualia of vision and hearing. Space-time consists of four dimensions: the three dimensions of space (height, width, length) plus a single dimension of time. But contemporary physics, supported by mathematics required to explain the results of new evidence obtained through experiments at very small spatial scales, believes there to be more than these four dimensions. Einstein himself, as part of his general theory of relativity attempting to unify electromagnetism and gravity, demonstrated that it takes ten numbers, tracking ten fields or dimensions, to precisely describe the workings of gravity in four dimensions.[2]

In 1926 a Swedish physicist, Oskar Klein, calculated the size of one of these dimensions as 10^{-30} cm, slightly above the Planck length limit of 10^{-33} cm.[3] In 1995, building upon the work of Einstein and Klein, a physicist in southern California, Edward Witten, proposed an eleven dimensional structure to the universe that has come to be known as "M-theory" (generally taken to stand for

---

[2] Yau, *The Shape of Inner Space*, p. 10.

[3] Klein, 1991, p. 110.

"membrane," "matrix," "master," and alternately, in a spirit of levity, as "mother," "monster," "mystery" and "magic").[4]

If space-time only accounts for four of eleven distinct dimensions, where might be the additional dimensions? Whitten developed his mathematics of M-theory upon the initial assumption that the fundamental constituents of reality must be tiny "strings" of Planck length (about 10^{-33} cm) that vibrate at various resonant frequencies.[5] But the topology, the conceptualized geometrical configuration of the missing seven dimensions, has been better depicted by Eugenio Calabi and Shing-Tung Yau in what is become known as the Calabi-Yau manifold, shown in Figure 1. Represented here is a geometric model of the missing seven dimensions at spatial scales of the Planck length. Note that each shade in the image represents a distinct dimension, other than the dimensions of space-time.

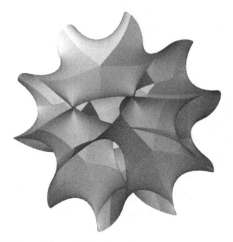

Figure 1. Calabi-Yau Manifold. Graphic by Ronhjones (2014). Retrieved from Wikimedia Commons.

---

[4] Duff, "M-theory (The Theory Formerly Known as Strings)."

[5] Yau, 124.

For purposes of this discussion, the Calabi-Yau manifold is a better representation of the "missing dimensions" than is the metaphorical geometry of a string, a gross simplification of the real topology, but required simply to make the mathematical computations possible. Thus within Bohm's implicate order, below spatial scales of 10^{-33} cm, the Calabi-Yau manifold models these missing seven dimensions, currently inaccessible to modern instruments of physics. As discussed previously, the Pribram-Bohm cosmology views the explicate order as ending at dimensions below the Planck length, below the surface of regions bounded by spherical shells of Planck length diameter. These boundary regions are also known as Planck holospheres or quantum black holes. Figure 2 shows the Calabi-Yau manifold in the context of the Pribram-Bohm topology.

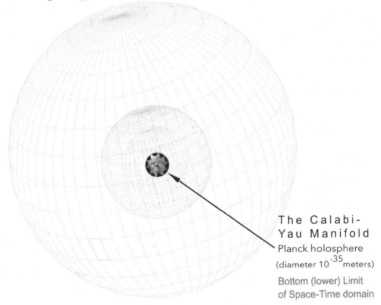

The Calabi-Yau Manifold
Planck holosphere
(diameter 10^{-35} meters)
Bottom (lower) Limit of Space-Time domain

Figure 2. Calabi-Yau Manifold superimposed on Planck holosphere. Graphic by author.

Rather than a string object, we see in Figure 2 is depicted at the Planck length the geometry of a Calabi-Yau manifold at the turbulent (multi-dimensional vibration) in the event horizon of a quantum black hole. Shing-Tung Yau, who proved the mathematical existence of the Calabi-Yau manifold, describes John Wheeler's concept of quantum foam in "the idea that what might appear to be a smooth, featureless object from a distance can look extremely irregular from close up."[6]

Fields, Frequency, and the Frequency Domain

An understanding of fields and frequency, their measurement and dynamics, are of central importance to an understanding of the holoflux field of consciousness applies electromagnetics in space-time to tune the mind. Pribram's experimental data convinced him that vision and other sensory systems operate through a holographic process, and developed what he termed the holonomic brain theory, postulating the importance of the *frequency domain*:

> Essentially, the theory reads that the brain at one stage of processing performs its analyses in the *frequency domain*. . .a solid body of evidence has accumulated that the auditory, somatosensory, motor, and visual systems of the brain do in fact process, at one or several stages, input from the senses in the *frequency domain*.[7]

It was Michael Faraday (1791–1867) who first conceived of the reality of an invisible electromagnetic "field" during his observation of magnetic lines of force

---

[6] Yau, pp. 315–14.

[7] Karl Pribram, "What the Fuss is All About," in *The Holographic Paradigm and Other Paradoxes*, ed. Ken Wilber (Boulder: Shambhala, 1982), 27–34.

around a conductor carrying a direct current.[8] But while Faraday had the ability to conceptualize a certain ontological reality, he did not have sufficient mathematical training to formalize the dynamics of his theorized field. Thus it was James Clerk Maxwell (1831–1879) who in 1861, through a series of interlocking equations, subsequently known as the "Maxwell equations," was able to model the dynamics of electric and magnetic energy, in waves of various frequencies, flowing through space–time in an ocean of vibrating flux.[9]

Figure 3. James Clerk Maxwell at Trinity College, Cambridge. Graphic by Tjlaxs (2005). Public domain image published in the US before 1923. Retrieved from Wikimedia Commons.

His discovery was a mathematical one, based upon his development of a set of four interlocking partial differential equations with which he was able to predict the dynamics of electric charges and how they are generated by oscillating magnetic fields. Ironically, though Maxwell's equations predicted electromagnetic waves, their existence was not accepted as real until nearly 25 years later, when Heinrich Hertz (1857–1894) experimentally detected

---

[8] Crease, *The Great Equations*, 135.

[9] Cook, *The Theory of the Electromagnetic Field*.

electromagnetic waves.[10] Nevertheless, Hertz was forever in awe of the equations that led him to his discovery, and here he speaks, with almost mystical reverence, of the "wisdom" that he has found in Maxwell's equations:

> One cannot escape the feeling that these mathematical formulae have an independent existence and an intelligence of their own, that they are wiser than we are, wiser even than their discoverers, that we get more out of them than was originally put into them.[11]

In the 1800s, frequencies were measured in units of "Cycles Per Second," a convention which was adopted for many decades into the twentieth century. With the development of quantum mechanics, it was realized that units of frequency often needed to be dimensionless for certain calculations to make sense. In 1930, a dimensionless frequency unit named, appropriately, "Hertz," was adopted by the International Electrotechnical Commission, officially replacing the misleading concept implied in units of "cycles per second."[12] Karl Pribram, commenting on the confusion, here suggests using the term "spectral density" in lieu of the term "frequencies":

> When we deal with a spectrum of frequencies per se, we often substitute the term "spectral density" to avoid a common confusion that Gabor pointed out in his paper: non mathematicians, even physicists, often think of frequencies as occurring only in time, but when mathematicians deal with vibrations as in the

---

[10] Hertz, *Electric Waves*.

[11] E. T. Bell, *Men of Mathematics*, 16.

[12] Ruppert, *History of the International Electrotechnical Commission*.

Fourier transform, frequencies are described as composing spectra and devoid of space and time.[13]

Perhaps Pribram is reacting here to the confusion in terminology that has muddled some critics of Pribram's holographic paradigm, leading them to believe that frequency by definition (as units of cycles per second) can only exist in space–time. Here for example, Ken Wilber exhibits this fallacy, apparently misled by the term "cycles/second," in his dismissal of Pribram's holographic paradigm:

> The transform of "things" into "frequencies" is not a transform of space/time objects into space/time frequencies. Frequency does not mean "no space, no time"; it means cycles/second or space per time. To read the mathematics otherwise is more than a quantum leap; it is a leap of faith.[14]

Sine Wave and Frequency in the Motion of an Exoplanet

It is useful to visualize the path of a sine wave in nature. Assume we are measuring the brightness of an exoplanet circling around a distant star, and that we are viewing it almost edge-on to its planar orbit. When the planet is closest to us, it will be brightest, and when it is on the opposite side of its central star, it will appear maximally dim, being at its furthest distance from our viewing point. If we were to plot the intensity of this visual image of an exoplanet over the period during which it makes one orbital cycle, it would appear, graphed on two-dimensional Cartesian coordinates, as the sine wave in Fig. 4. Where the

---

[13] Pribram, *The Form Within*, 105.

[14] Wilber, *The Holographic Paradigm*, 181.

graph crosses the zero axis corresponds to the exoplanet being at right angles to its star and our vantage point.

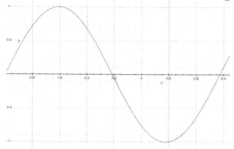

Figure 4. A sine wave. Graphic by author.

According to the Bohr model of atomic theory, electrons spinning around their nuclei emit similar sine wave patterns as they orbit, and accordingly, space–time is replete with sinusoidal electromagnetic waves of an almost infinite number of different frequencies, corresponding to orbiting photons.[15] The frequency of radiation emitted is the inverse of the orbital time; for example, an orbit that takes one second to complete would emit electromagnetic radiation of 1 Hz, while an orbit of an electron with smaller radii would exhibit a higher frequencies of radiant of energy. The closer to the center, they faster the orbit and the less time expired.

The wavelength of a sine wave is a measurement of the distance, in space, between any two points with the same phase of a frequency, such as between troughs, crests, or zero crossing in the same direction. Figure 5 illustrates the concept of wavelength, depicting the graph of a sine of wavelength λ.

<hr>

[15] Baggott, *The Quantum Story*, 30.

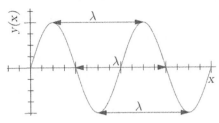

Figure 5. Wavelength. Graphic by Richard F. Lyon (2009). Reprinted under the terms of a Creative Commons Attribution ShareAlike 3.0 Unported license. Image retrieved from Wikimedia Commons.

Frequency charts of radiant electromagnetic energy are commonly depicted as a spectrum displayed on two-dimensional Cartesian coordinates with named ranges, some of which are listed in Table 3, "Ranges of the Electromagnetic Field."

Table 3

Ranges of the Electromagnetic Field

Named range	Approximate wavelengths	Frequency (Hz)
Radio waves	10^3 or 1 kilometer	10^6
Microwaves	10^0 or 1 meter	10^9
Infrared	10^{-8} meters	10^{13}
Visible light	10^{-9} meters	10^{14}
UV rays	10^{-10} meters	10^{16}
X rays	10^{-11} meters	10^{18}
Gamma rays	10^{-12} meters	10^{19}

Note. Data adapted from Benenson et al., *Handbook of Physics*, 227.

The ubiquitous word "heat" tends to confuse an actual phenomenon with an epiphenomenon. The actual the sensation termed "heat" is a measure of human neurosensory reaction to the physically radiant energy phenomenon of electromagnetic energy interacting with neurons in the skin cells. The actual energy in question is invisible electromagnetic radiation in the infrared band of the spectrum. Similarly, when we use the word "light," we tend to fall into the same potentially specious obfuscation. The term "light," like heat, pertains to the bio-sensory phenomenon of visual perception, while the primary phenomenon is actually pure radiant electromagnetic energy, precisely the same kind of energy as "heat," though of a higher frequency (a shorter wavelength) in the significantly broader electromagnetic spectrum.[16]

What is less commonly considered is that the living human body itself broadcasts a unique, narrow spectrum of electromagnetic radiation in the infrared band of radiation.[17] Wien's Law (Equation 1 below) states that the maximum electromagnetic wavelength generated by a theoretically perfect "black body" at a specific given temperature is calculated as follows:

$$\lambda_{\mathbf{max}} = \frac{b}{T}$$

Equation 1. Wien's Law.[18] Graphic by author.

Here "b" in the equation is a constant discovered by Wilhelm Wien in 1893 and is equal to 2.897768551×10^3 m K, and T is the temperature.[19] If we substitute the core

---

[16] Feynman, Leighton, and Sands, *The Feynman Lectures on Physics,* 72.

[17] Becker and Selden, *The Body Electric: Electromagnetism and the Foundations of Life.*

[18] Feynman, Leighton, and Sands. *The Feynman Lectures on Physics, Vol. 1,* 74.

[19] Crease, *The Great Equations,* 128.

human body temperature of 98.6 F for *T*, we obtain the maximum wavelength to be **9.34 micrometers**. Electromagnetic energy vibrating at this wavelength lies within the range of the infrared region, just below the range of humanly visible light frequencies. It is of interest to note that human bodies generate electromagnetic radiation at frequencies with a wavelength approximately five times smaller than the diameter of a human hair, but the approximate size of a human red blood cell.[20]

Energy vibrating in the infrared band of radiation also has a unique relationship with water. It is within the infrared range that water molecules exhibit their maximum transmittance or transparency to electromagnetic radiation, as can be seen in Fig. 6, "Water Response to Infrared Electromagnetic Radiation." A sharp dip in the absorption coefficient of atmospheric water vapor can be seen in the graph at about 10 microns on the horizontal axis. Such a dip is what communication engineers call a "passband." Earth's atmosphere exhibits a passband to radiation in the 10 micron range, the infrared. What is important to note here is that this atmospheric passband closely matches the human peak wavelength of electromagnetic radiation, previously calculated as 9.34 microns.[21]

---

[20] Becker, *Cross Currents: The Perils of Electropollution.*

[21] Warren and Brandt, "Optical Constants of Ice from the Ultraviolet to the Microwave," 1049.

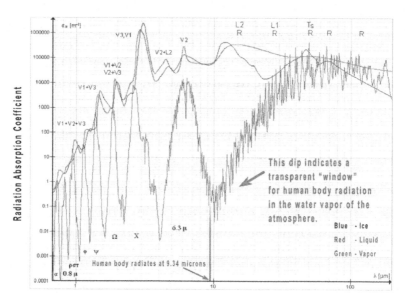

Figure 6. Water response to infrared radiation.[22] *Annotation added by author to image by Darekk2 (2012). Reprinted under the terms of Creative Commons Attribution ShareAlike 3.0 Unported. Image retrieved from Wikimedia Commons.*

If the dynamics of human consciousness has evolved to broadcast and receive in this frequency range, then it would be a very convenient thing indeed that the atmosphere of our planet is transparent in this range. At 9.34 microns, the atmosphere with its gasses and water molecules does not absorb our radiant energy but allows it to pass relatively unrestricted and unattenuated in the biosphere. The passbands of the Earth's atmosphere can be seen in a graph of atmospheric electromagnetic opacity by wavelength, plotted by NASA (Fig. 7).

---

[22] Water absorption spectrum; absorption coefficient for water—liquid (red line), vapor (green) and ice (blue) between 667 nm and 200 μm (red and most important part of infrared).

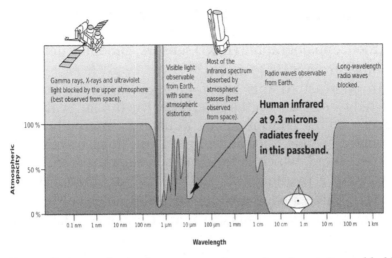

Figure 7. Atmospheric electromagnetic opacity. Annotation added by author to NASA image by Mysid (2008). Public domain image retrieved from Wikimedia Commons.

As early as 1939 military engineers began exploiting the fact that the electromagnetic radiation emitted by human bodies is transparent to the atmosphere. This realization enabled them to develop electro-optic night vision devices specifically to observe human infrared radiation travelling through the atmosphere at wavelengths between 9 and 10 microns.[23]

Water molecules themselves, as vapor in the atmosphere, may act as magnetically resonant dipole "highways," providing infrared channels and currents in the air, even among the clouds, for electromagnetic bio-networking around Earth's globe. Such bio-communication possibilities for human infrared radiation have been widely ignored in the neuroscience community, where such energy is understandably dismissed as "heat," or "noise," or "random thermodynamic activity," while the focus continues to be primarily upon the search for bands of

---

[23] Clark, *Photography by Infrared—Its Principles and Applications*, 78.

111

human consciousness within the relatively slow, "brain-wave" frequency regions recorded by scalp-affixed electroencephalographic (EEG) sensors, generally detected in a range from 8 Hz to 50 Hz.[24]

In contrast to this low frequency range (8–50 Hz) detected by sensors on the exterior of the human scalp, the human body continuously radiates, internally and externally, in the "thermal infrared" or "long-wavelength infrared" band, which is tuned to wavelengths from 8–15 microns, in a frequency range from 27–30 THz (1 THz = 10^{12} Hz). Table 4 compares the detected ranges of human EEG frequency and human infrared frequency. The much higher frequency band of infrared as compared to EEG would translate to vast differences in information processing and storage capacity, discussed later in this chapter.

Table 4

Frequency Range: Brain Waves Versus Plasma Waves

Wave type	Frequency (Hz)
EEG "Brain Wave"	$0.8–5 \times 10^{1}$ Hz
Infrared "Plasma Wave"	$2.7–3 \times 10^{13}$ Hz

Note. Data adapted from Nunez. *Brain, Mind*, 216. Author's table.

Potentially significant biological correlations can now be established. The human emission of radiation wavelengths in the 9.34 micron range not only lies within the infrared band, but also is dimensionally the same size as the prokaryote (basically, a bacteria), believed to be the first living organism on planet Earth.[25] This human electromagnetic wavelength of 9.34 microns also matches

---

[24] Nunez, *Brain, Mind, and the Structure of Reality*, 104–5.

[25] Zimmer, "Origins: On the Origin of Eukaryotes," 667.

the average diameter of human blood capillaries, the smallest of the body's circulatory structures, on the average 8–10 microns in diameter; it has been estimated that there are approximately 25,000 miles of capillaries within each adult human body.[26] To appreciate the significance of the correlation of the human infrared radiation wavelength and the inner diameter of the human capillary system, it is important to understand the concept of waveguides in communication engineering.

Waveguides have been used for over a century, both commercially and in research, to channel and guide vibrating energy of specific limited frequency ranges. It was discovered late in the nineteenth century that circular metallic tubes, or hollow metal ducts, similar to A/C ventilation ducts, but much smaller, could be used to channel and guide either sound vibrations in air, or electromagnetic energy in air or vacuum. Without the waveguide, the vibrational energy field is transmitted in all directions, which may be visualized as magnetic lines, arrows emerging from a point at the center of an expanding sphere.

This energy disperses outwardly, the magnetic vectored arrowheads pushing into the inside of an infinitely expanding sphere. A waveguide, however, constrains the magnetic component of the wave-front of vibrating energy to one specific linear direction, in parallel with the center of the waveguide, and thus, conceptually, the wave itself loses very little power while confined to propagate down the center of the waveguide, like a stream of water emerging from the pinprick of a large, taut, water balloon.[27]

In the mid-twentieth century, scientists began to develop microwave devices for radar and high information, bi-directional communication. In general, the inner

---

[26] Romanes, *Cunningham's Textbook of Anatomy*, 840.

[27] Dorf, *The Electrical Engineering Handbook*.

dimension (diameter) of the waveguide must be of the same order of magnitude as the wavelength being "guided." Electrical engineers during World War II developed radar technology by using metal waveguides to channel, modulate, and detect frequencies in the microwave band.[28]

Contemporary data networks are increasingly channeled through optical waveguides using the properties of thin transparent fiber optic materials. High-speed network optical fibers currently used in the global Internet confine light to their core, most commonly using a glass fiber with a core diameter of 8–10 microns, designed for laser communication in the near infrared, the frequency band in which the ubiquitous carbon dioxide laser (CO_2 laser) emits coherent radiation. The CO_2 laser is one of the most widely used lasers due to its ability to reliably operate at the highest-power efficiency currently found among laser systems.[29]

Perhaps it should not come as a surprise then that living human blood cells operate within their energy environment in the same infrared band as does our Internet data, and that the blood system is saturated with carbon dioxide gas. If conscious information processing in the human bio-system uses electromagnetic energy as a medium, then waveguide networks might also be identified within human physiology. Dimensional analysis, developed in the following section, would indicate the possibility of two systems of enclosed, tubular structures that might act as waveguides for bands of networked human electromagnetics.

A recent proposal by the University of California Los Angeles neuroscientist N. J. Woolf goes so far as to identify

---

[28] Ibid.

[29] Kachris, Christoforos, Bergman, and Tomkos, *Optical Interconnects for Future Data Center Networks*.

the site of memory storage in the locus of microtubule channels:

> Most contemporary models of consciousness posit synaptic activity as the primary basis of consciousness . . . . The view I propose is that the site of memory storage is not within the synapse, but in the sub-synaptic zone, in the microtubules of the dendrite shaft . . . the logic to this proposal is that the synapse is a channel transmitting information, much like a radio receiver . . . . In this analogy, the receiving channel is the synapse or spine.[30]

Such waveguides might be a function of any one or several systems within the physiology of the human body, such as the blood capillary system, the microtubule system, or other structures as indicated in Fig. 8.

---

[30] Woolf, "Microtubules in the Cerebral Cortex," 83–84.

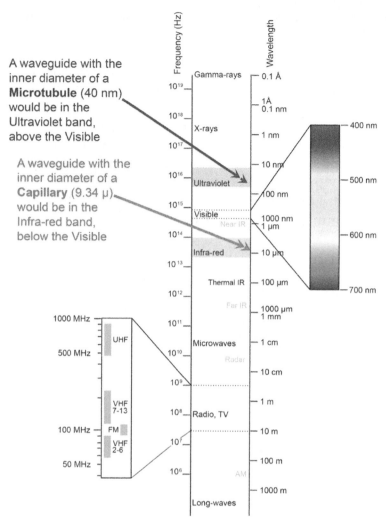

Figure 8. Microtubules and capillaries as waveguides. Annotations by author; graphic by Jahoe (2012). Reprinted under the terms of a Creative Commons Attribution ShareAlike 2.5 Generic license. Image retrieved from Wikimedia Commons.

Dimensional evidence indicates that good candidate ranges for testing the electromagnetic field component of consciousness can be found in the infrared spectrum. This

116

region lies just below the threshold of the visible spectrum that is picked up by eye cone structures.[31]

Human body temperature ranges from a minimum of 68.0 F. (hypothermia with loss of consciousness) to a maximum of 106.7 F (maximum core brain temperature before death). Applying Wien's Law to this range of human body temperature reveals the bandwidth of human electromagnetic wavelengths (Fig. 9) to span the range from 9.88 to 9.11 microns, completely within the dimensions of human blood capillaries taken as waveguides.

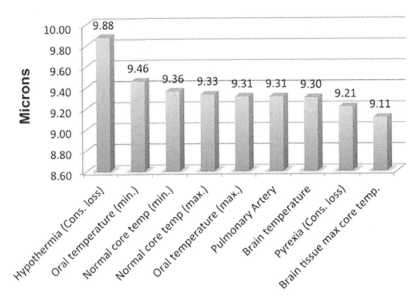

Figure 9. Human electromagnetic wavelength.[32] Graphic by author.

---

[31] Oyster, *The Human Eye: Structure and Function.*

[32] Data from Geiger, Aron, and Todhunter, *The Climate Near the Ground*, 452.

Converting from wavelength, this range is equivalent to a frequency range of 30.3 gigahertz to 32.0 gigahertz, an enormously wide band compared to, for example, the FM radio frequency band, ranging from 87.0 to 88.1 MHz. Over 1000 equivalent FM radio stations could be easily broadcast within the human infrared radiation band, with no overlapping interference.[33]

Assuming that electromagnetic energy in the infrared range networks consciousness within the human body, where might we search to detect such activity? One approach in the search for an infrared component of consciousness would be to monitor the dynamics of an infrared spectrum emanating from and external to the human body in an attempt to detect information laden photons escaping the body as modulated infrared radiation.

> Interestingly, because biologic materials are transparent to light in the near-infrared region of the light spectrum, transmission of photons through organs is possible.[34]

Another approach would be to search for infrared energy signals flowing as patterns within physiological waveguide channels within the human body. The ubiquitous blood capillary system, for example, with typical inner diameters of 10 microns, is a likely candidate to be acting as an electromagnetic waveguide. Capillaries provide a ready-made network infrastructure within which the flow and resonance of a modulated infrared energy plasma might be discovered.

---

[33] Calculations in this paragraph use Wien's Law to convert wavelength to frequency.

[34] Cohn, *Near-Infrared Spectroscopy: Potential Clinical Benefits in Surgery*, 323.

In conclusion, there are numerous structural systems within human physiology that may involve consciousness as modulated electromagnetic energy, and these have thus far been largely neglected in the widespread, possibly erroneous assumption that brain structures and neurons are the only feasible biological structures involved with consciousness. While it is a widely held assumption that consciousness is an epiphenomenon generated through the action of neuronal spikes in the brain, we propose here that consciousness may involve tuning the mind in the frequency domain at subquantum dimensions and ultra-high frequencies, and that such an approach might offer new directions in research that may yet to be explored through cutting-edge projects in the near future, freeing up resources that seem to be focused exclusively on low frequency activity among neurons.

References

Alabiso, Carlo, and Ittay Weiss. 2015. *A Primer on Hilbert Space Theory: Linear Spaces, Topological Spaces, Metric Spaces, Normed Spaces, and Topological Groups.* New York: Springer.

Allaby, Michael, and Ailisa Allaby, eds. 1999. "Telluric Current." In *A Dictionary of Earth Sciences.* 2nd ed. New York: Oxford University.

Amuecki. 2008. "File:Resonance.png" (graphic file). November 11, 2015. Wikimedia Commons..

Aur, Dorian, and Mandar S. Jog. 2010. *Neuroelectrodynamics: Understanding the Brain Language.* Amsterdam: IOS Press.

Averse. 2007. "File:Diplexer1.jpg" (graphic file). November 13, 2015. Wikimedia Commons. Retrieved from https://en.wikipedia.org/wiki/Microwave#/media/File:Diplexer1.jpg.

Baggott, Jim. 2011. *The Quantum Story: A History in 40 Moments.* New York: Oxford University.

Bain, George Grantham. 2011. "File:Niels_Bohr_Date_Unverified_LOC.jpg" (graphic file). November 28, 2015. Wikimedia Commons. Retrieved from https://commons.wikimedia.org/wiki/File:Niels_Bohr_Date_Unverified_LOC.jpg.

Becker, Robert O., and Gary Selden. 1985. *The Body Electric: Electromagnetism and the Foundation of Life.* New York: Harper.

Bekenstein, Jacob D. 1973. "Black Holes and Entropy." *Physical Review* 7 (8): 2333–46.

Bell, E. T. 1937. *Men of Mathematics*. New York: Simon and Schuster.

Bell, J. S. 1987. *The Speakable and Unspeakable in Quantum Mechanics*. Cambridge: Cambridge University.

Benenson, Walter, John W. Harris, Horst Stocker, and Lutz Holger, eds. 2006. *Handbook of Physics*. New York: Springer Science.

Berg, Jerome S. 2008. *Broadcasting on the Short Waves, 1945 to Today*. London: McFarland & Company.

Bergson, Henri. 1911. *Creative Evolution*. Translated by Arthur Mitchell. New York: Henry Holt.

Bisson, Terry. 1990. "They're Made Out of Meat." *Omni Magazine* 13 (7): 42–45. New York: General Media.

Blakeslee, Douglas, ed. 1972. *The Radio Amateur's Handbook*. Newington, CT: The American Radio Relay League.

Blinkov, S. M. and I. I. Glezer. 1968. *The Human Brain in Figures and Tables. A Quantitative Handbook*. New York: Plenum.

Block, Ned. 2007. *Consciousness, Function, and Representation: Collected Papers, Vol. 1*. Cambridge: The MIT Press.

Bohm, David. 1951. *Quantum Theory*. New York: Prentiss-Hall.

———. 1952. "A Suggested Interpretation of the Quantum Theory in Terms of 'Hidden Variables,' Vol. 1." *Physical Review* 85 (2): 166–93. Retrieved from http://fma.if.usp.br/~amsilva/Artigos/p166_1.pdf
.

———. 1965. *The Special Theory of Relativity*. Philadelphia: John Benjamins.

———. 1978. "The Enfolding-Unfolding Universe: A Conversation with David Bohm." In *The Holographic Paradigm and Other Paradoxes: Exploring the Leading Edge of Science*, edited by Ken Wilber, 44–104. Boulder, CO: Shambhala.

———. 1980. *Wholeness and the Implicate Order*. London: Routledge.

———. 1985. *Unfolding Meaning: A Weekend of Dialogue with David Bohm*. London: Routledge.

———. 1986. "The Implicate Order and the Super-Implicate Order." In *Dialogues with Scientists and Sages: The Search for Unity*, edited by Renée Weber, 23–49. New York: Routledge.

———. 1987a. "Hidden Variables and the Implicate Order." In *Quantum Implications: Essays in Honour of David Bohm*, edited by B. J. Hiley and F. David Peat, 33–45. London: Routledge.

———. 1989. "Meaning and Information." In *The Search for Meaning: The New Spirit in Science and Philosophy*, edited by Paavo Pylkkänen, 43–85. Northamptonshire, England: The Aquarian Press.

———. 1990. *Beyond Limits: A Full Conversation with David Bohm*. Interview by Bill Angelos for Dutch public television. Posted March 5, 2011. Retrieved from http://bohmkrishnamurti.com/beyond-limits/

———. 1990. "A New Theory of the Relationship of Mind and Matter." *Philosophical Psychology* 3 (2): 271–86.

Bohm, David, and Basil J. Hiley. 1993. *The Undivided Universe: An Ontological Interpretation of Quantum Theory.* London: Routledge.

Bohm, David, and J. Krishnamurti. 1985. *The Ending of Time: Where Philosophy and Physics Meet.* New York: Harper Collins.

Bohm, David, and J. Krishnamurti. 1999. *The Limits of Thought: Discussions between J. Krishnamurti and David Bohm.* London: Routledge.

Bohm, David, and F. David Peat. 1987. *Science, Order, and Creativity.* London: Routledge.

Bohm, David, and R. Weber. 1982. "Nature as Creativity." *ReVision* 5 (2): 35–40.

Booth, J. C., S. A. Koren, and Michael A. Persinger. 2005. "Increased Feelings of the Sensed Presence and Increased Geomagnetic Activity at the Time of the Experience During Exposures to Transcerebral Weak Complex Magnetic Fields." *International Journal of Neuroscience* 115 (7): 1039–65.

Born, Irene, trans. 1971. *The Born–Einstein Letters: Friendship, Politics and Physics in Uncertain Times.* New York: Macmillan.

Borsellino, A., and T. Poggio. 1972. "Holographic Aspects of Temporal Memory and Optomotor Responses." *Kybernetik* 10 (1): 58–60.

Brigham, E. O. 2002. *The Fast Fourier Transform.* New York: Prentice-Hall.

Broughton, S. A., and K. Bryan. 2008. *Discrete Fourier Analysis and Wavelets: Applications to Signal and Image Processing.* New York: Wiley.

Browder, Andrew. 1996. *Mathematical Analysis: An Introduction.* New York: Springer-Verlag.

Bruskiewich, Patrick. 2014. *Max Planck and Black-Body Radiation*. Vancouver: Pythagoras Publishing.

Carr1, Bernard J. and Steven B. Giddings. 2005. "Quantum Black Holes." *Scientific American* 292 (5): 30–35.

Cazenave, Michel, ed. 1984. *Science and Consciousness: Two Views of the Universe, Edited Proceedings of the France-Culture and Radio-France Colloquium, Cordoba, Spain*. Oxford: Pergamon.

Chalmers, David J. 1995. "Facing Up to the Problem of Consciousness." *Journal of Consciousness Studies* 2 (3): 200–19.

———. 2010. *The Character of Consciousness*. New York: Oxford University.

Chen, Frances F. 2006. *Introduction to Plasma Physics and Controlled Fusion: Vol 1. Plasma Physics*. 2nd ed. New York: Springer.

Chomsky, Noam. 2000. *New Horizons in the Study of Language and Mind*. Cambridge, England: Cambridge University.

Clark, Walter. 1939. *Photography by Infrared—Its Principles and Applications*. New York: John Wiley & Sons.

Cohn, Stephen M., 2007. "Near-Infrared Spectroscopy: Potential Clinical Benefits in Surgery." *Journal of the American College of Surgeons* 205 (2): 322–32. doi: http://dx.doi.org/10.1016/j.jamcollsurg.2007.02.024.

Collister, Rupert Clive. 2010. *A Journey in Search of Wholeness and Meaning*. New York: Peter Lang.

Cook, David M. 2002. *The Theory of the Electromagnetic Field*. Englewood Cliffs, NJ: Prentice-Hall.

Crease, Robert P. 2008. *The Great Equations: Breakthroughs in Science from Pythagoras to Heisenberg*. New York: W. W. Norton.

Darekk2. 2012. "File:Water_infrared_absorption_coefficient_large.gif" (graphic file). November 28, 2015. Wikimedia Commons. Retrieved from https://en.wikipedia.org/wiki/File:Water_infrared_absorption_coefficient_large.gif.

Darling, David J. 2004. *The Universal Book of Mathematics: From Abracadabra to Zeno's Paradoxes*. Hoboken, NJ: Wiley.

Deacon, Terrence W. 2010. "What Is Missing from Theories of Information." In *Information and the Nature of Reality: From Physics to Metaphysics*, edited by Paul Davies and Niels Henrik Gregersen, 123–42. Cambridge, England: Cambridge University.

———. 2012. *Incomplete Nature: How Mind Emerged from Matter*. New York: W. W. Norton.

De Valois, Karen K., and Russell L. De Valois. 1988. *Spatial Vision*. New York: Oxford University.

Dennett, Daniel C. 1991. *Consciousness Explained*. New York: Back Bay Books.

Dewey, B. 1985. *The Theory of Laminated Spacetime*. Inverness, CA: Bartholomew.

Dewynne, Dustin. 2012. "File:Dualism-vs-Monism.png" (graphic file). November 27, 2015. Wikimedia Commons. Retrieved from https://commons.wikimedia.org/wiki/File:Dualism-vs-Monism.png.

Differenxe. 2010. "File:Sawtooth_Fourier_Analysys.svg"
(graphic file). October 22, 2015. Wikimedia
Commons. Retrieved from
http://commons.wikimedia.org/wiki/File:Sawtoot
h_Fourier_Analysys.svg.

Dorf, Richard C., ed. 1997. *The Electrical Engineering
Handbook.* 2nd ed. Boca Raton, FL: CRC Press.

Drachman, David A. 2005. "Do We Have Brain to Spare?"
Neurology 64 (6): 2004–5. doi:
http://dx.doi.org/10.1212/01.WNL.0000166914.3
8327.BB.

Dunwell, Frances F. 1980. *The Hudson: America's River.*
New York: Columbia University.

Edelman, Gerald M., and Giulio Tononi. 2000. *A
Universe of Consciousness: How Matter Becomes
Imagination.* New York: Basic Books.

Edmondson, Amy C. 1987. *A Fuller Explanation: The
Synergetic Geometry of R. Buckminster Fuller.*
Boston: Birkhäuser.

Einstein, Albert. 1979. *Autobiographical Notes.* Peru, IL:
Carus.

Eliot, Thomas Stearns. 1943. *Four Quartets.* New York:
Harcourt Brace.

———. 1976. *Collected Poems 1909–1962.* New York:
Harcourt Brace.

Fechner, Gustav Theodor. 1946. *Religion of a Scientist:
Selections from Gustav Theodor Fechner.* New
York: Pantheon.

Ferrer, Jorge, and Jacob Sherman, eds. 2008. *The
Participatory Turn: Spirituality, Mysticism,
Religious Studies.* Albany: State University of New
York.

126

Feuerstein, Georg. 1987. *Structures of Consciousness: The Genius of Jean Gebser—An Introduction and Critique*. Lower Lake, CA: Integral.

Feynman, Richard, Robert Leighton, and Matthew Sands. 1964. *The Feynman Lectures on Physics, Vol. 1.* Reading, MA: Addison-Wesley.

Fields, R. Douglas. 2009. *The Other Brain*. New York: Simon & Schuster.

Flanagan, Owen. 1997. "Conscious Inessentialism and the Epiphenomenalist Suspicion." In *The Nature of Consciousness: Philosophical Debates*, edited by Ned Block, Owen Flanagan, and Güven Güzeldere, 357–73. Cambridge, MA: MIT Press.

Fourier, Jean Baptiste Joseph. 1822. *The Analytic Theory of Heat*. Paris: Firmin Didot Père et Fils.

Fulvio314. 2013. "File:Coat_of_Arms_of_Niels_Bohr.svg" (graphic file). November 28, 2015. Wikimedia Commons. Retrieved from https://commons.wikimedia.org/wiki/File:Coat_of_Arms_of_Niels_Bohr.svg.

Gabor, Dennis. 1946. "Theory of Communication." *Journal of the Institute of Electrical Engineers* 93: 429–41.

Gao, Shan. 2014. *Dark Energy: From Einstein's Biggest Blunder to the Holographic Universe*. 2nd ed. Seattle, WA: Amazon Kindle Direct.

Garay, Luis J. 1995. "Quantum Gravity and Minimum Length." *International Journal of Modern Physics* 10 (2): 145–65.

Gebser, Jean. 1949. *The Ever-Present Origin: Part One: Foundations of the Aperspectival World*.

Translated by J. Keckeis. Stuttgart, Germany: Deutsche Verlags-Anstalt.

———. 1956 (1996). "Cultural Philosophy as Method and Venture." Translated by Georg Feuerstein. *Integrative Explorations: Journal of Culture and Consciousness* 3 (1): 77–82. Retrieved from http://static1.squarespace.com/static/535ef5d8e4 b0ab57db4a06c7/t/541f74a0e4b0394ddbf5a040/ 1411347616917/integrative_explorations_3.pdf.

Geiger, Rudolf, Robert H. Aron, and Paul Todhunter. 2003. *The Climate Near the Ground.* Lanham, MD: Rowman and Littlefield.

Gidley, Jennifer. 2007. "The Evolution of Consciousness as a Planetary Imperative: An Integration of Integral Views." *Integral Review* 3 (5): 4–226. Retrieved from http://integral-review.org/pdf-template-issue.php?pdfName=issue_5_gidley_the_evolutio n_of_consciousness_as_a_planetary_imperative. pdf.

Glatzmaier. 2007. "File:Geodynamo_Between_Reversals.gif" (graphic file). November 12, 2015. Wikimedia Commons. Retrieved from https://commons.wikimedia.org/wiki/File:Geody namo_Between_Reversals.gif.

Globus, Gordon G. 2006. *The Transparent Becoming of World: A Crossing Between Process Philosophy and Quantum Neurophilosophy.* Philadelphia: John Benjamins.

Goswami, Amit. 2000. *The Visionary Window: A Quantum Physicist's Guide to Enlightenment.* Wheaton, IL: Quest Books.

Gott, J. Richard III, Mario Jurić, David Schlegel, and Fiona Hoyle. 2005. "A Map of the Universe." *The Astrophysics Journal* 624 (2): 463–514.

Gray, Henry. 1918. "File:Gray754.png" (graphic file). October 31, 2015. Wikimedia Commons. Retrieved from https://commons.wikimedia.org/wiki/File:Gray754.png.

Haas, Jonathan. 2012. "File:Neurons_uni_bi_multi_pseudouni.svg" (graphic file). October 31, 2015. Wikimedia Commons. Retrieved from http://commons.wikimedia.org/wiki/File:Neurons_uni_bi_multi_pseudouni.svg.

Haisch, Bernard. 2010. *The Purpose-Guided Universe: Believing in Einstein, Darwin, and God.* Pompton Plains, NJ: New Page Books.

Hameroff, Stuart R. 2015. "Is Your Brain Really a Computer, or Is It a Quantum Orchestra?" *Huffington Post*, July 9. Retrieved from http://www.huffingtonpost.com/stuart-hameroff/is-your-brain-really-a-co_b_7756700.html.

Hameroff, Stuart, and Roger Penrose. 1996. "Conscious Events as Orchestrated Space-Time Selections." *Journal of Consciousness Studies* 3 (1): 35–53.

Hameroff, Stuart R., Travis J. A. Craddock, and Jack A. Tuszynski. 2014. "Quantum Effects in the Understanding of Consciousness." *Journal of Integrative Neuroscience* (13) 2: 229–52. doi:10.1142/S0219635214400093.

Harnad, Stevan. 1994. "Why and How We Are Not Zombies." *Journal of Consciousness Studies* 1 (1): 18–23.

Havelka, D., M. Cifra, O. Kucera, J. Pokorny, and J. Vrba. 2011. "High-frequency Electric Field and Radiation Characteristics of Cellular Microtubule Network." *Journal of Theoretical Biology* 286 (7): 31–40.

Herculano-Houzel, Suzana. 2009. "The Human Brain in Numbers: A Linearly Scaled-up Primate Brain." Frontiers in Human Neuroscience (3) 31: 1–11. doi: 10.3389/neuro.09.031.2009

Hertz, Heinrich. 1893. *Electric Waves: Being Researches On the Propagation of Electric Action with Finite Velocity Through Space.* London: MacMillan.

Hiley, B. J., and F. David Peat, eds. 1987. *Quantum Implications: Essays in Honour of David Bohm.* London: Routledge.

Hiley, B. J., and F. David Peat, eds. 1987. "The Development of David Bohm's Ideas from the Plasma to the Implicate Order." In *Quantum Implications: Essays Honour of David Bohm,* edited by B. J. Hiley and F. David Peat, 1–32. London: Routledge.

Horne, Alistair. 1962. *The Price of Glory: Verdun 1916.* New York: St. Martin's Press.

Howell, Kenneth B. 2001. *Principles of Fourier Analysis.* Boca Raton, FL: Chapman & Hall.

Ishikawa, Hiroaki, and Wallace F. Marshall. "Ciliogenesis: Building the Cell's Antenna." *Nature Reviews Molecular Biology* 12 (4): 222-34. dos:10.1038/nrm3085

Jahoe. 2012. "File:Electromagnetic-Spectrum.png" (graphic file). November 28, 2015. Wikimedia Commons. https://commons.wikimedia.org/wiki/File:Electromagnetic-Spectrum.png.

Jbarta. 2014. "File:Max_Planck_1878.GIF" (graphic file). November 28, 2015. Wikimedia Commons. Retrieved from https://commons.wikimedia.org/wiki/File:Max_Planck_1878.GIF.

Jibu, Mari, and Kunio Yasue. 1995. *Quantum Brain Dynamics and Consciousness*. Philadelphia: John Benjamins.

———. 2003. "Quantum Brain Dynamics and Quantum Field Theory." In *Brain and Being: At the Boundary Between Science, Philosophy, Language and Arts*, edited by Gordon Globus, Karl Pribram, and Giuseppe Vitiello, 267–90. Philadelphia: John Benjamins.

Johnston, Sean F. 2006. *Holographic Visions: A History of New Science*. New York: Oxford University.

Joye, S. 2016. *The Pribram–Bohm holoflux theory of consciousness: An integral interpretation of the theories of Karl Pribram, David Bohm, and Pierre Teilhard de Chardin* (Doctoral dissertation). ProQuest Dissertations and Theses database. (UMI No. 1803306323).

Jung, C. G. 1968. *Psychology and Alchemy*. Vol. 12 of *The Collected Works of C. G. Jung*. Edited and translated by Gerald Adler and R. F. C. Hull. 2nd ed. Princeton, NJ: Princeton University.

———. (1946) 1969. "On the Nature of the Psyche." In Vol. 8 of *The Collected Works of C. G. Jung*, translated by R. F. C. Hull, 159–234. 2nd ed. Princeton, NJ: Princeton University.

Kachris, Christoforos, Keren Bergman, and Ioannis Tomkos. 2012. *Optical Interconnects for Future Data Center Networks*. New York. Springer.

Kafatos, Menas, Rudolph E. Tanzi, and Deepak Chopra. 2011. "How Consciousness Becomes the Physical Universe." *Journal of Cosmology* (14): 1318–1328. Retrieved from http://journalofcosmology.com/Consciousness14 0.html.

Köhler, Wolfgang. 1940. *Dynamics in Psychology: Vital Applications of Gestalt Psychology*. New York: W. W. Norton.

———. 1969. *The Task of Gestalt Psychology*. New Jersey: Princeton University.

Köhler, Wolfgang, and Mary Henle. 1971. *The Selected Papers of Wolfgang Köhler*. New York: W. W. Norton.

Kuehn, Kerry. 2014. A Student's Guide Through the Great Physics Texts, Vol. 1: The Heavens and The Earth. New York: Springer.

Kuo, Franklin. 1962. *Network Analysis and Synthesis*. New York: John Wiley & Sons.

Lashley, Karl. 1951. "An Examination of the Electric Field Theory of Cerebral Integration." *Psychological Review* 58: 123–36.

———. 1950. "In Search of the Engram." *Symposium of the Society for Experimental Biology* 4: 454–82.

László, Ervin. 2006. *Science and the Re-Enchantment of the Cosmos: The Rise of the Integral Vision of Reality*. Rochester, VT: Inner Traditions.

———. 2014a. *The Immortal Mind: Science and the Continuity of Consciousness beyond the Brain*. Rochester, VT: Inner Traditions.

———. 2014b. *The Self-Actualizing Cosmos: The Akasha Revolution in Science and Human Consciousness*. Rochester, VT: Inner Traditions.

Leckie, Robert. 1987. *Delivered from Evil: The Saga of World War II*. New York: Harper & Row.

Leith, Emmet N., and J. Upatnieks. 1962. "Reconstructed Wavefronts and Communication Theory." *Journal of the Optical Society of America* 52 (10): 1123–30.

———. 1965. "Photography by Laser." *Scientific American* 212 (6): 24–35.

Lilly, John. 1967. *The Mind of the Dolphin: A Nonhuman Intelligence*. New York: Doubleday.

———. 1977. *The Deep Self: Consciousness Exploration in the Isolation Tank*. New York: Simon & Schuster.

Livio, Mario. 2003. *The Golden Ratio: The Story of Phi, the World's Most Astonishing Number*. New York: Broadway Books.

Lundqvist, Stig, ed. 1992. *Nobel Lectures, Physics 1971–1980*. Singapore: World Scientific.

Lyon, Richard F. "File:Sine_wavelength.svg" (graphic file). November 22, 2015. Wikimedia Commons. Retrieved from https://commons.wikimedia.org/wiki/File:Sine_wavelength.svg.

MacKenna, Stephen. 1992. *Plotinus: The Enneads*. New York: Larson Publications.

Malinski, Tadeusz. 1960. *Chemistry of the Heart*. Ohio: Biochemistry Research Laboratory. Retrieved from http://hypertextbook.com/facts/2003/IradaMuslumova.shtml

Mandelbrot, Benoit. 1986. "Fractals and the Rebirth of Iteration Theory." In *The Beauty of Fractals: Images of Complex Dynamical Systems*, by H.-O. Peitgen and P. H. Richter, 151–60. Berlin: Springer-Verlag.

McCraty, Rollin. 2003. *The Energetic Heart: Bioelectromagnetic Interactions Within and Between People*. Boulder Creek, CA: Institute of HeartMath.

McCraty, Rollin, M. Atkinson, D. Tomasino, and R. T. Bradley. 2009. "The Coherent Heart: Heart–Brain Interactions, Psychophysiological Coherence, and the Emergence of System-Wide Order." *Integral Review* 5 (9): 10–115.

McCraty, Rollin, Annette Deyhle, and Doc Childre. 2012. "The Global Coherence Initiative: Creating a Coherent Planetary Standing Wave." *Global Advances in Health and Medicine* 1 (1): 64–77. Retrieved from https://www.heartmath.org/assets/uploads/2015/01/gci-creating-a-coherent-planetary-standing-wave.pdf.

McFadden, Johnjoe. 2002a. "The Conscious Electromagnetic Information (CEMI) Field Theory: The Hard Problem Made Easy." *Journal of Consciousness Studies* 9 (8): 45–60.

———. 2002b. "Synchronous Firing and Its Influence on the Brain's Electromagnetic Field: Evidence for an Electromagnetic Field Theory of Consciousness." *Journal of Consciousness Studies* 9 (4): 23–50.

———. 2006. "The CEMI Field Theory." In *The Emerging Physics of Consciousness*, edited by Jack A. Tuszynski, 385–404. Berlin: Springer-Verlag.

———. 2007. "Conscious Electromagnetic Field Theory." *NeuroQuantology* 5 (3): 262–70.

134

McGinn, Colin. 1997. "Consciousness and Space." In *Explaining Consciousness: The Hard Problem*, edited by Jonathan Shear, 97–108. Boston: MIT.

McIntosh, Steve. 2007. *Integral Consciousness and the Future of Evolution*. St. Paul, MN: Paragon House.

Merrell-Wolff, Franklin. 1973. *The Philosophy of Consciousness Without an Object: Reflections on the Nature of Transcendental Consciousness*. New York: Julian Press.

Milonni, Peter W., and Joseph E. Eberly. 2010. *Laser Physics*. Hoboken, NJ: John Wiley & Sons.

Morgan, Conway Lloyd. 1978. *Emergent Evolution: Gifford Lectures, 1921–22*. New York: Simon & Schuster.

Morin, Edgar. 1999. *Seven Complex Lessons in Education for the Future*. Translated by Nidra Poller. Paris: UNESCO.

Mysid. 2008. "File:Atmospheric_electromagnetic_opacity.svg" (graphic file). November 28, 2015. Wikimedia Commons. https://commons.wikimedia.org/wiki/File:Atmospheric_electromagnetic_opacity.svg.

National Multiple Sclerosis Society. n.d. "Cerebrospinal Fluid (CSF)." Retrieved from http://www.nationalmssociety.org/Symptoms-Diagnosis/Diagnosing-Tools/Cerebrospinal-Fluid-(CSF).

Netter, F. H. 1972. *A Compilation of Paintings of the Normal and Pathologic Anatomy of the Nervous System*. Summit, NJ: CIBA.

Neville, Katherine. 1992. "Saral and David Bohm, Prague, June 1992" (photograph). Retrieved from http://www.karlpribram.com/photos/.

Nilson, Arthur R., and J. L. Hornung. 1943. *Practical Radio Communication: Principles, Systems, Equipment, Operation, Including Very High and Ultra High Frequencies and Frequency Modulation.* 2nd ed. New York: McGraw-Hill.

Nishikawa, K., and M. Wakatani. 2000. *Plasma Physics.* Berlin: Springer-Verlag.

Nunez, Paul L. 2010. *Brain, Mind, and the Structure of Reality.* New York: Oxford University.

Oates, B. 1971. *Celebrating the Dawn: Maharishi Mahesh Yogi and the TM Technique.* New York: Putnam Books.

Ouspensky, P. D. 1949. *In Search of the Miraculous: Fragments of an Unknown Teaching.* London: Harcourt.

Oyster, Clyde W. 1999. *The Human Eye: Structure and Function.* Sunderland, MA: Sinauer Associates.

Peat, F. David. 1997. *Infinite Potential: The Life and Times of David Bohm.* Reading, MA: Addison-Wesley.

Pelekanos. (1478) 2007. "File:Serpiente_alquimica.jpg" (graphic file). File uploaded April 10 by Carlos Adanero. Wikimedia Commons. Retrieved from https://commons.wikimedia.org/wiki/File:Serpie nte_alquimica.jpg.

Penfield, Wilder. 1975. *The Mystery of the Mind: A Critical Study of Consciousness and the Human Brain.* Princeton, NH: Princeton University.

Penrose, Sir Roger. 1989. *The Emperor's New Mind: Concerning Computers, Minds and the Laws of Physics*. New York: Oxford University.

Penrose, R., Stuart Hameroff, and S. Kak, eds. 2011. *Consciousness and the Universe: Quantum Physics, Evolution, Brain & Mind* (Contents selected from Volumes 3 and 14, *Journal of Cosmology*). Cambridge: Cosmology Science.

Persinger, Michael A. 2014. "Schumann Resonance Frequencies Found Within Quantitative Electroencephalographic Activity: Implications for Earth-Brain Interactions." *International Letters of Chemistry, Physics and Astronomy* 30: 24–32. doi:10.18052/www.scipress.com/ILCPA.30.24.

Pizzi, Rita, Giuliano Strini, Silvia Fiorentini, Valeria Pappalardo, and Massimo Pregnolato. 2010. "Evidences of New Biophysical Properties of Microtubules." In *Artificial Neural Networks*, edited by Seoyun J. Kwon. New York: Nova Science Publishers, 1–17. Retrieved from https://air.unimi.it/retrieve/handle/2434/167480 /168890/evidences.pdf.

Planck, Max. 1901. "On the Law of Distribution of Energy in the Normal Spectrum." *Annalen der Physik*. 309 (3): 553–63.

Pockett, Susan. 2000. *The Nature of Consciousness: A Hypothesis*. Lincoln, NE: Writers Club.

———. 2007. "Difficulties with the Electromagnetic Field Theory of Consciousness: An Update." *NeuroQuantology* 5 (3): 271–75. Retrieved from http://www.neuroquantology.com/index.php/jou rnal/article /view/136/136 (login required).

Pribram, Karl H. 1962. "The Neuropsychology of Sigmund Freud." In *Experimental Foundations of Clinical*

Psychology, edited by Arthur J. Bachrach, 442–68. New York: Basic Books.

———. 1971. *Languages of the Brain: Experimental Paradoxes and Principles in Neuropsychology*. Englewood Cliffs, NJ: Prentice-Hall.

———. 1982. "What the Fuss is All About." In *The Holographic Paradigm and Other Paradoxes*, edited by Ken Wilber, 27–34. Boulder: Shambhala.

———. 1984. "Mind, Brain and Consciousness: The Organization of Competence and Conduct." In *Science and Consciousness: Two Views of the Universe*, edited by Julian Davidson and Richard Davidson, 115–32. New York: Springer.

———. 1990. "Prolegomenon for a Holonomic Brain Theory." In *Synergetics of Cognition*, edited by H. Haken, 150–84. Berlin: Springer-Verlag.

———. 1991. *Brain and Perception: Holonomy and Structure in Figural Processing*. Hillsdale, NJ: Lawrence Erlbaum.

———. 1994. "What Is Mind that the Brain May Order It?" In *Proceedings of Symposia in Applied Mathematics: Proceedings of the Norbert Wiener Centenary Congress, Vol. 52*, edited by V. Mandrekar and P. R. Masani, 301–29. Providence, RI: American Mathematical Society.

———. 2004a. "Brain and Mathematics." In *Brain and Being: At the Boundary Between Science, Philosophy, Language and Arts*, edited by Gordon Globus, Karl Pribram, and Giuseppe Vitiello, 215–40. Philadelphia: John Benjamins.

———. 2004b. "Consciousness Reassessed." *Mind and Matter* 2 (1): 7–35.

———. 2011. "Karl Pribram: Bibliography." Retrieved from http://www.karlpribram.com/bibliography/.

———. 2013. *The Form Within: My Point of View.* Westport, CT: Prospecta Press.

Pribram, Karl H., A. Sharafat, and G. Beekman. 1984. "Frequency Encoding in Motor Systems." In *Human Motor Actions: Bernstein Reassessed,* edited by H. T. A. Whiting, 121–56. Amsterdam: Elsevier Science Publishers.

Prigogine, Ilya. 2015. *Modern Thermodynamics: From Heat Engines to Dissipative Structures.* Hoboken, NJ: John Wiley & Sons.

Pylkkänen, Paavo. 2007. *Mind, Matter, and the Implicate Order.* New York: Springer.

Radhakrishnan, Sarvepalli, ed. 1952. *History of Philosophy Eastern and Western, Vol. 2.* London: George Allen & Unwin.

Ramon y Cajal, Santiago. 2007. "File: Purkinje_cell_by_Cajal.png" (graphic file). January 30, 2016. Wikimedia Commons. Retrieved from https://commons.wikimedia.org/wiki/File:Purkinje_cell_by_Cajal.png.

Rendek, Kimberly N., Raimund Fromme, Ingo Grotjohann, and Petra Fromme. 2013. "Self-Assembled Three-Dimensional DNA Nanostructure." *Acta Crystallographica Section F: Structural Biology and Crystallization Communications* 69 (2): 141–46. doi:10.1107/S1744309112052128.

Rescher, Nicholas, ed. 1991. *G. W. Leibniz's Monadology: An Edition for Students.* Pittsburgh: University of Pittsburgh.

Ringbauer, M., B. Duffus, C. Branciard, E. G. Cavalcanti, A. G. White, and A. Fedrizzi. 2015. "Measurements On the Reality of the Wavefunction." *Nature Physics* 11 (2): 249–254. doi:10.1038/nphys3233.

Romanes, G. J., ed. 1964. *Cunningham's Textbook of Anatomy*. 10th ed. New York: Oxford University.

Romary. 2006. "File:Come pariou.jpg" (graphic file). January 29, 2016. Wikimedia Commons. Retrieved from https://commons.wikimedia.org/wiki/File:Come_pariou.jpg.

Rose, D. 2006. Consciousness: Philosophical, Psychological and Neural Theories. New York: Oxford University.

Ruhenstroth-Bauer, Gerhard. 1993. "Influence of the Earth's Magnetic Field on Resting and Activated EEG Mapping in Normal Subjects." *International Journal of Neuroscience* 73 (3): 331–49.

Runehov, Anne, and Luis Oviedo, eds. 2013. *Encyclopedia of Sciences and Religions*. Dordrecht, Netherlands: Springer Netherlands.

Ruppert, L. 1956. *History of the International Electrotechnical Commission*. Geneva: Central Bureau of the IEC.

Samson, Paul R., and David Pitt, eds. 1999. *The Biosphere and Noosphere Reader: Global Environment, Society and Change*. New York: Routledge.

Schrock, Karen. 2007. "An Opera Singer's Piercing Voice Can Shatter Glass." *Scientific American*, August 23. Retrieved from http://www.scientificamerican.com/article/fact-or-fiction-opera-singer-can-shatter-glass/

Sentman, Davis D. 1995. "Schumann Resonances." In *Handbook of Atmospheric Electrodynamics, Vol. 1*, edited by Hans Volland, 267–96. Boca Raton, FL: CRC Press.

Shannon, C. E. 1948. "A Mathematical Theory of Communication." *Bell System Technical Journal* 27: 623–56.

Sheldrake, Rupert. 1981. *A New Science of Life: The Hypothesis of Morphic Resonance*. Rochester, VT: Park Street.

———. 1988. *The Presence of the Past: Morphic Resonance and the Habits of Nature*. New York: Times Books.

———. 1989. *Morphic Resonance: The Nature of Formative Causation*. Rochester, VT: Park Street.

Skrbina, David. 2007. *Panpsychism in the West*. Cambridge, MA: MIT Press.

Smolin, Lee. 2013. *Time Reborn*. London: Penguin Books.

Sperry, Roger W., N. Miner, and R.E. Myers. 1955. "Visual Pattern Perception Following Subpial Slicing and Tantalum Wire Implantations in the Visual Cortex." *Journal of Comparative and Physiological Psychology* 48 (1): 50–58.

Squire, Larry R., ed. 1998. *The History of Neuroscience in Autobiography, Vol. 2*. London: Academic Press.

Stanford Daily. 1977. "Scientists to Speak." 172 (2): 8.

Stapp, Henry P. 2009. *Mind, Matter, and Quantum Mechanics*. 3rd ed. New York: Springer-Verlag.

Steiner, Rudolf. 1959. *Cosmic Memory: Prehistory of Earth and Man*, translated by K. E. Zimmer. San Francisco: Harper & Row.

Stuart, C.I.J., Y. Takahashi, and H. Umezawa .1979. "Mixed System Brain Dynamics: Neural Memory as a Macroscopic Ordered State." *Foundations of Physics* (9): 301–7.

Susskind, Leonard. 2008. *The Black Hole War: My Battle with Stephen Hawking to Make the World Safe for Quantum Mechanics.* New York: Little, Brown and Company.

Svdmolen. 2005. "File:Red_White_Blood_cells.jpg" (graphic file). November 12, 2015. Wikimedia Commons. Retrieved from https://en.wikipedia.org/wiki/File:Red_White_Blood_cells.jpg.

Taimni, I. K. 1969. *Man, God and the Universe.* Madras, India: The Theosophical Society.

Talbot, Michael. 1992. *The Holographic Universe.* New York: Harper Collins.

Telsa, Faraday. 2014. "File:Assembly_of_microscale_beads_on_Faraday_waves.gif" (graphic file). February 7, 2016. Wikimedia Commons.

Teilhard de Chardin, Pierre. (1944) 1976. "Centrology: An Essay in a Dialectic of Union." In *Activation of Energy,* translated by René Hague, 97–127. London: William Collins Sons.

Tjlaxs. 2005. "File:YoungJamesClerkMaxwell.jpg" (graphic file). November 28, 2015. Wikimedia Commons. https://commons.wikimedia.org/wiki/File:YoungJamesClerkMaxwell.jpg.

Turgeon, Mary Louise. 2004. *Clinical Hematology: Theory and Procedures.* Baltimore, MD: Lippincott Williams & Wilkins.

142

Tudzynski, P., T. Correia, and U. Keller. 2001. "Biotechnology and Genetics of Ergot Alkaloids." *Applied Microbiology and Biotechnology*, 57: 593–605. doi:10.1007/s002530100801.

Tuszyński, Jack A., ed. 2006. *The Emerging Physics of Consciousness*. New York: Springer-Verlag.

Van Dokkum, Pieter G., and Charlie Conroy. 2010. "A Substantial Population of Low-Mass Stars in Luminous Elliptical Galaxies." *Nature* 468 (7326): 940–42. doi:10.1038/nature09578.

Vejvoda, Stanislav. 2003. *17th International Conference on Structural Mechanics in Reactor Technology*. Prague, Czech Republic: Czech Standard Institute.

Walker, J. Samuel. 2004. *Three Mile Island: A Nuclear Crisis in Historical Perspective*. Berkeley: University of California Press.

Warren, Stephen G., and Richard E. Brandt. 2008. "Optical Constants of Ice from the Ultraviolet to the Microwave: A Revised Compilation." *Journal of Geophysical Research*, 113 (D14): 1047–57.

Wasson, Tyler, and Gert Brieger. 1987. *Nobel Prize Winners: A Biographical Dictionary*. New York: H. W. Wilson.

Weber, Renée. 1982. "The Physicist and the Mystic—Is a Dialogue Between Them Possible?" In *The Holographic Paradigm and Other Paradoxes: Exploring the Leading Edge of Science*, edited by Ken Wilber, 187–214. Boulder, CO: Shambhala.

Weisenberger, Drew. n.d. "Jefferson Lab Questions and Answers: How Many Atoms Are There in the World?" Retrieved January 20, 2016 from http://education.jlab.org/qa/mathatom_05.html

Wheeler, John Archibald. 1990. *Information, Physics, Quantum: The Search for Links*. Austin, TX: University of Texas.

———. 1990. *A Journey into Gravity and Spacetime*. New York: Scientific American.

———. 1998. Geons, Black Holes, and Quantum Foam: A Life in Physics. New York: W. W. Norton.

Whitehead, Alfred North. 1978. *Process and Reality: An Essay in Cosmology*. *Gifford Lectures*, 1927–28. New York: Simon & Schuster.

Wick, Manfred, Wulf Pinggera, and Paul Lehmann. 2003. *Clinical Aspects and Laboratory Iron Metabolism*. Vienna, Austria: Springer-Verlag.

Wiener, Norbert. 1948. *Cybernetics or Control and Communication in the Animal and the Machine*. Cambridge, MA: MIT Press.

Wilber, Ken, ed. 1982. *The Holographic Paradigm and Other Paradoxes: Exploring the Leading Edge of Science*. Boulder, CO: Shambhala.

———, ed. 1985. Quantum Questions: Mystical Writings of the World's Great Physicists. Boston: Shambhala.

———. 1996. *A Brief History of Everything*. Boston: Shambhala.

———. 1997. *Integral Spirituality: A Startling New Role for Religion in the Modern and Postmodern World*. Boston: Integral Books.

Wiltschko, Wolfgang, and Roswitha Wiltschko. 2008. "Magnetic Orientation and Magnetoreception in Birds and Other Animals." *Journal of Comparative Physiology A: Neuroethology, Sensory, Neural, and Behavioral Physiology* 191 (8): 675–93. doi:10.1007/s00359-005-0627-7.

Wiseman, Howard M., Fuwa Maria, Shuntaro Takeda, Marcin Zwierz, and Akira Furusawa. 2015. "Experimental Proof of Nonlocal Wavefunction Collapse for A Single Particle Using Homodyne Measurements." *Nature Communications* 6: 192–203. Retrieved from http://www.nature.com/ncomms/2015/150324/ncomms7665/full/ncomms7665.html.

Wong, Eva. 1997. *The Shambhala Guide to Taoism.* Boston: Shambhala.

Woolf, N. J. 2006. "Microtubules in the Cerebral Cortex: Role in Memory and Consciousness." In *The Emerging Physics of Consciousness*, edited by Jack A. Tuszyński, 49–94. New York: Springer-Verlag.

Yau, Shing-Tung, and Steve Nadis. 2010. *The Shape of Inner Space: String Theory and the Geometry of the Universe's Hidden Dimensions.* New York: Basic Books.

Zimmer C. 2009. "Origins: On The Origin of Eukaryotes." *Science* 325 (5941): 666–68.

Zizzi, Paola. 2006. "Consciousness and Logic in a Quantum Computing Universe." In *The Emerging Physics of Consciousness*, edited by Jack A. Tuszyński, 457–81. New York: Springer-Verlag.

Index

Notes

Made in the USA
Columbia, SC
02 July 2021

41308861R00095